# I'm a
# Lucky Guy

# I'm a
# Lucky Guy

JOSEPH F. CULLMAN 3RD

Library of Congress Cataloging-in-Publication Data

Cullman, Joseph F. (Joseph Frederick).
I'm a lucky guy / Joseph F. Cullman 3rd
    p.   cm
Includes index.
ISBN 0-934037-48-5
1. Cullman. Joseph F. (Joseph Frederick), 1912– .
2. Businesspeople—United States—Biography.
3.Tobacco industry—United States—History.
4. Philip Morris Incorporated—History.
I. Title.
HD9140.C843A3  1998
338.7 ' 6797 ' 092—dc21
[B]                                                     98-13468
                                                            CIP

Unless otherwise credited, all photographs
are courtesy of the author.

Maps created by Eddie Ocampo

*This is dedicated to
my mother, Frances Wolff Cullman,
and my dad, Joseph F. Cullman Jr.
I am a lucky guy to have had such
wonderful parents.*

# Contents

# Acknowledgments

THIS BOOK STARTED OUT as a purely business chronicle; we asked Professor Bob Sobel of Hofstra to help, and indeed he did. It then became a more personal narrative. Jim Ramsay of Philip Morris, my editor, was invaluable. Elizabeth Cain, assistant editor, performed brilliantly day after day with great patience. Paul Hunter brought his legendary skills to helping arrange my life in pictures. Alex Holtzman brought his great legal expertise to the table on many occasions. Chuck Wall's legal overview was most constructive. Among my former associates at Philip Morris, George Weissman, Hamish Maxwell, Cliff Goldsmith, and John Murphy all made important contributions and refreshed my memory many times. Alan Mogel's designs were important. Robin Newman, my administrative assistant, and Anne Durante, my former executive secretary, performed beyond the call of duty. My wife, Joan, selected the cover art and gave me critical encouragement as I wrote; she also supplied great family photos.

# Preface

THIS IS MY STORY OF MY LIFE—my personal life, my business life, my family life, and my life as an active conservationist with a passion for wildlife, nature and the outdoors plus my active participation in the world of golf and tennis.

I grew up in a tobacco family. My father, Joe Cullman Jr., "Mr. Junior," and my grandfather "Joe Senior" were tobacco men. That was their world, and it became my world after graduation from Yale in 1935.

I started out as a clerk in a Schulte Cigar store, then went on to training in a Cuban cigar factory, then worked as a Webster Cigar "missionary" man, then was a marketing man for Webster. I had no way of even dreaming that I would end up after World War II first at a tiny company called Benson & Hedges, which made Parliament cigarettes, then—after Philip Morris bought B&H—that I would be involved in developing a new popular-priced filter cigarette called Marlboro.

I went over to Philip Morris in 1954, when it bought B&H. I became CEO in 1957. Philip Morris went from sixth in the industry in 1954 to the number one tobacco company in the world today, and Marlboro became one of the world's most powerful trademarks. I stepped down as CEO in 1978. Sales grew from about $300 million when I joined PM, to $6.5 billion in 1978 when I became chairman of the executive committee. In 1983, when I became chairman emeritus —which I still am—sales had reached $13.3 billion. PM had sales of over $70 billion in 1997.

I could not have dreamed that I would become head of the premier company in tobacco, nor could I have dreamed that the tobacco industry would come under such violent attack.

When I got out of college, the major tobacco companies, such as R. J. Reynolds and American Tobacco, were super-blue-chip companies on the New York Stock Exchange, with highly respected leadership like Bowman Gray of RJR and Paul Hahn of American.

Today the industry is under siege in the United States. The industry has made major changes in its product over the past forty years to meet demand for a milder product—filters, lowered tar and nicotine, blend changes. The industry has made great changes in its marketing methods. More are on the way.

Millions of people in the United States and the world still enjoy smoking. Philip Morris's job is to make a superior product and satisfy the desires of those smokers everywhere. To me, smoking is a personal choice that adults should be able to make when they have been adequately informed of the possible risks of smoking—and they have been. Warning messages have been appearing on packs and in ads for over thirty years.

This book is not designed to address the smoking and health question. There is no simple, easy answer. We have changed our product to meet changing demand. We are changing our marketing. Our job is to be a responsible cigarette manufacturer, a good corporate citizen, and I feel we are that and have been that.

This book is about my life, my experiences, and the people and things I hold dear. If you read it, I think you will understand why I consider myself so lucky.

# I'm a Lucky Guy

# CHAPTER ONE

# *Growing Up*

Courage, hard work, self-mastery, and intelligent effort are all essential to successful life.

—Theodore Roosevelt
America and the World War

Character, in the long run, is the decisive factor
in the life of an individual and of nations alike.

—Theodore Roosevelt
American Ideals

I WAS A VERY LUCKY GUY from the very beginning of my life:
marvelous parents, good genes, lucky in love, lucky in business, and lucky when a Yale classmate had my orders
changed to report to Washington, D.C., in early 1941, instead of to a ship that was sunk with all hands lost in the
North Atlantic, lucky in the Navy, and lucky to be alive at
eighty-five.

An important part of my life has always been family,
with two great wives, great parents, an older sister, Nan, and
three younger brothers, Arthur, Edgar, and Lewis. My

mother, Frances Wolff Cullman, always called me her "salmon pink baby," because, as she told me near the end of her life, I was conceived on the rocky shores of a salmon river in Quebec—the Riviere St. Marguerite. Pretty good for someone who had been through polio at fourteen years of age. My mother was called Frank because she was so honest and forthright. She was very family oriented.

One of my earliest recollections is running away from home. I was six years old at the time and can't for the life of me remember why I did it. The year would have been 1918, since I was born April 9, 1912. My parents and I had a good relationship. In fact, they got along well with each of my siblings as well. I must have run away after an argument over one thing or another, or they might have forbidden me to do something. In any case, I stayed out all night and returned the next morning. Little was said about the episode, and I never did it again.

I have only a vague memory of World War I—not surprisingly, since it ended when I was six. But I do recall my uncle, Colonel Arthur Wolff, my mother's brother, taking me to see the returning troops marching up Fifth Avenue after the Armistice in the fall of 1918. Then there was the time in 1925 or thereabouts when we went to Washington and visited the White House, where I got to shake President Calvin Coolidge's hand. This wasn't the big deal it became later on: Coolidge would shake hands most days for an hour or so at the White House.

At the time of my birth my family was living in Far Rockaway, Long Island, New York, a seaside town that was a summer resort and a bucolic retreat from the city. Mother enjoyed life in the countryside; it made quite a change for the city girl she had been before her marriage. We did live in a town house in Manhattan during the winter, but during the summers and on some weekends the rest of the year we stayed in the Far Rockaway house. It was a large Dutch colonial fieldstone house designed by my uncle John Wolff, down the street from my grandfather's house. Dad went off to work weekday mornings while Mother took care of us.

The story of my family starts out with my great-grand-parents, whom I know from stories told me by my father and grandfather. My great grandfather, Ferdinand Kullman, Joe Cullman Sr.'s father, was one of the hordes of Germans who came to America in the wake of the failure of the liberal revolution of 1848 in Germany. Most of these immigrants were farmers and went to the Midwest, where there was already a sizable German-American population and where farmland was inexpensive. But Ferdinand Kullman and his brother, Heinrich, had not been farmers but wine merchants in the little town of Bingen-am-Rhein. They were wealthy, well-known, and sophisticated enough to know that conditions in their homeland were starting to deteriorate.

So they relocated to Frankfurt, and from there Ferdinand and his bride, Eva Pappenheim, took a ship to America, settling in Hoboken, New Jersey. There, Ferdinand entered the wine retailing business and also manufactured and sold cigars. There, too, their children, Joseph, Jacob (Jake), Lena, and Bella were born; they were joined, when Eva's sister and brother-in-law died, by their two orphaned cousins. So it was a large family, not too well off, but probably in much better circumstances than most people of the time.

Joseph Cullman (Ferdinand changed the spelling of the name to Americanize it), my grandfather, went to work at the age of fifteen at Egbert, Dills & Company, a cigar leaf tobacco merchant on Water Street at the tip of Manhattan Island. In this period, it was a highly competitive and active business, with many small and mid-sized firms, usually family controlled; there was no single commanding entity.

This was 1869, when tobacco was almost universally

used only by men, usually in the form of cigars and plug, sometimes as pipe tobacco and snuff, and rarely as cigarettes. That very same year the Sweet Caporal cigarette was produced by F. S. Kinney, one of the leaders in that small segment of the industry. Old-timers took little notice of cigarettes, and youngsters like Joe Senior thought the product had little future. He considered himself a cigar leaf man, and so he was for the rest of his life.

At that time Joe Senior was very handsome, with an overwhelming, German kind of personality; he was rather short, but solidly built, with a big head, and a big mustache. He had a lot of charm, and was very friendly toward his grandchildren. I remember how he would sit at the piano on holidays, playing "Tannenbaum," which was his favorite song. He loved music, and my grandparents had regular Monday night seats at the Academy of Music not far from their home. The Academy was the city's leading opera house until the Metropolitan Opera opened in 1883, whereupon they attended the Met as well.

What I remember most about my grandfather was that he knew the cigar business and the cigar leaf business very well. He had a reputation for being gregarious and engaging, which he was, but he was also a formal person and could be very serious. Near the end of his life he took me aside and said, "Let me tell you something. Stay out of the tobacco business. It's dying." By "tobacco" he meant cigars, of course, because to him, cigars were the only form that mattered.

Grandfather believed cigars were healthy and wholesome. Cigarettes were another matter entirely. When I was young, he advised me not to smoke them until I was at least twenty-one years old, because they would stunt my growth. He offered me a fine automobile if I refrained from cigarettes till then. But when I got to be nineteen, the car was reduced to a Ford, and when I was close to twenty-one, it became a motorcycle.

I learned from my father that in his youth, Joe Senior was ambitious, intelligent, and hardworking, a combination that permitted him to rise swiftly at Egbert, Dills (which soon became Fox, Dills & Company). Before he had reached the age of twenty, he was the firm's crackerjack salesman, and he knew all the ins and outs of the cigar leaf business. On his twentieth birthday, in recognition of his importance to the business, he was made a partner, and in 1876 the firm got a new name: Fox & Cullman.

In 1881 Joe Senior, then twenty-seven years old, married the lady who became my grandmother: Zillah Stix, an intelligent woman who was a member of a wealthy Cincinnati family. They went on a European honeymoon, during which they visited the German Kullmans and saw the sights in Paris—and Joe Senior explored the famous cigar leaf markets in Amsterdam, where leaf imported from Dutch Sumatra and Java was bought and sold. Joe Senior was seeking contacts and new ideas, and he succeeded in both. In those days the Amsterdam tobacco auctions were quite important and well attended. The tobacco was of a high grade but cost less than Cuban tobacco, so cigar makers monitored the situation in Amsterdam carefully. Merchants who knew what they were up to could reap great profits by buying and selling leaf. Joe Senior knew about this, and now he learned more at first hand.

The newlyweds returned home to a modest house on West Fourteenth Street in New York, then a popular residential neighborhood, which today is for the most part commercial and rather run-down. Mr. Dills, who was running Fox & Cullman, became quite ill and had to neglect the business. So Joe Senior stepped in to run the day-to-day operations, concentrating on restoring the company's prosperity and cementing relations with the Amsterdam merchants.

Dills died the following year while returning home from

a leaf-buying trip to Holland, whereupon Joe Senior's brother, Jake, came into the business along with Albert Rosenbaum, a knowledgeable and well-regarded dealer in cigar tobacco. The firm was now renamed Cullman and Rosenbaum. That wasn't the only reason 1882 was important to the family: on June 25 of that year my father, Joseph Frederick Cullman Junior, was born. Nine years later, Zillah Cullman gave birth to another son, Howard, who was to become an important figure in several areas. My uncle Howard chaired the New York Port Authority and was a well-known Broadway "angel" with his silent partner, Dad. Their most famous early investment was *Life with Father*, which set a record for longevity.

My Cullman grandparents were both Jews, who around this time became active in the New York Society for Ethical Culture. This organization had been founded in 1876 by Felix Adler. While a rabbinical student in Berlin, Adler became interested in philosophy. Later, he decided to create a movement devoted, as the name implies, to the study and promulgation of what he considered an ethical life, which included concerns with philanthropy.

As Adler put it, Ethical Culture was for "fathers and mothers who felt the need both for themselves and for their children for something to take the place of the consecrating influence of the old religions." So their children would attend Ethical Culture classes. When it was my generation's turn, that's where I went, as did my brothers and sister.

Ethical Culture School was most enjoyable and I had many friends. It was close to our house, so I was able to walk to and from school. The most memorable teacher there—for me, at least, but I suspect for others as well—was John Fielding Elliot. He was a very inspirational fellow who bore a slight resemblance to Averell Harriman—tall, distinguished, handsome. I suppose what I derived from the school was its philosophy. It made a lot of sense for people who did not believe strongly in religion, but thought we should treat each other well. Even then I thought Ethical Culture was a good, rational adjustment to the unreality of certain aspects of organized religion.

Now that Cullman and Rosenbaum was in strong hands, Joe Senior was free to roam the Dutch markets annually, usually with his wife and son. Sometimes before and sometimes after the obligatory trip to Frankfurt for a month with the family, they would go to Amsterdam for the tobacco auctions. My grandfather had wide interests but, like many dedicated businessmen, he tended to relate events in the broader world to the way they might affect his affairs.

Jake assumed Joe Senior's duties in his absence. The brothers were very close and completely different from each other. Jake was a quiet, diffident man, slight, with a clubfoot. He loved to study business, philosophy, and the classics, while my grandfather was more a man of action.

In Washington, 1890 was a busy year. The Sherman Antitrust Act was passed, signaling a new phase in the antitrust movement, and the Sherman Silver-Purchase Act also became law, troubling those who feared for the soundness of the currency, meaning the businessmen. I don't think my grandfather would have been too concerned about these measures since he was relatively small fry. But a third bill, the McKinley Tariff, passed on October 1, 1890, was another matter entirely.

I thought about this a half-century later when I was majoring in history in college, listening to a professor talk about post–Civil War tariffs, and how they rose with the passage of each new measure. The 1883 tariff lowered rates somewhat, but the McKinley Tariff raised the average level to a shade less than 50 percent, the highest since the Civil War. Big businessmen wanting protection saw this as a boon, while consumers and farmers were dismayed. Joe Senior was neither a big businessman nor a farmer, but he instantly knew that once this measure went into effect it would disturb the tobacco import business.

What followed was one of those legends many families have, which they repeat over and over again, and pass on from generation to generation. Joe Senior borrowed a large sum from his father-in-law and took the next ship to Amsterdam. News of the tariff on tobacco arrived before he did, and speculators and dealers had purchased large amounts of Sumatra and Java leaf in anticipation of a price rise.

Prices were high by the time Joe Senior got to the market, but he thought they would go higher still. So he purchased hundreds of thousands of pounds of Sumatra wrapper leaf, using the borrowed money as a deposit. He then returned to New York to await the arrival of the shipment, which came through customs a day and a half before the new tariff schedule went into effect.

Joe Senior had earlier tried to borrow $3 million from National City Bank, which handled the affairs of Cullman and Rosenbaum. Percy R. Pyne, the bank's president, told him that under existing law the bank couldn't lend more than $500,000 to any one person.

Hearing this, my grandfather thought he would be unable to pay for the shipment; he would not only lose his deposit, but be liable for additional costs and penalties. Seeing his dismay, Mr. Pyne quickly added, "But the law only says that my bank cannot lend you more than half a million. It doesn't say that *I* cannot."

So with the $500,000 from the bank and the $2.5 million from Mr. Pyne, Joe Senior paid for and took possession of that shipment. He was then able to sell the Sumatra leaf tobacco at substantially higher prices than he had paid for it, return the loans, and still have a tidy net profit.

The Cullmans were originally what I would call middle-class. They now became upper-middle-class, and could afford to transform the company into a family business. In 1892 Joe and Jake bought out Rosenbaum, Jake was made a full partner, and the company was renamed Cullman Brothers (it was the direct ancestor of today's Culbro Corporation). The company continued to thrive and grow. Within a decade it would have tobacco warehouses in Wisconsin and Connecticut, where we also had farms, and would be selling to some of the nation's most important cigar companies. Culbro was listed on the New York Stock Exchange until 1997 and remains a leader in the cigar field, with General Cigar and such brands as Macanudo, Partagas, and Garcia y Vega. My younger brother Edgar is chairman there and behind him is his son, Edgar Junior, as CEO.

When I was in college, I learned that the 1890s were a dismal decade economically and politically, not at all the so-called Gay Nineties portrayed in the movies I saw at the time. It was a time of depression and political upheaval, but none of this seemed to touch the Cullmans. In 1895, a particularly bad year, the family moved uptown, to a large new brownstone at 39 West Seventy-first Street. They had a maid, a cook, and a horse and carriage—none of which, at that time, was unusual for a family that deemed itself merely "comfortable."

By then Joe Junior was thirteen years old and enrolled at a very fine private school, Dr. Sachs's Collegiate Institute. Dad used to tell me stories of what it was like to grow up in New York at that time. Dr. Sachs, he recalled, was a large German with an inordinate love of Goethe's *Faust* and the history of art, subjects he taught himself. Dad took courses in Latin, Greek, and everything else required to get him into a good college. There seemed to be no question he would make it, since Dr. Sachs boasted that no student graduated from his school ever failed to pass the entrance examinations.

Joe Junior was an average student, not what in my day we called a grind. Classes were held from nine A.M. to four-fifteen P.M., with an hour off for lunch. After school my father would play ice hockey during the winter and run track in the spring in Central Park. Twice a month in the autumn and early winter, there would be football games at Hoguet's Field at 219th Street and Riverside Drive, to which he was driven in a horse-drawn omnibus. Dad was a short, stocky man, who as a boy was quite attractive. In after-school activities he became adept at hockey, and was quarterback and captain of the school's football team.

In 1900 my father entered Yale. In those years students spent more time on athletics, fraternities, and partying than studies. It was the heyday of the "Gentleman's C" and the "absentminded professor"; Joe Junior ran no risk of being considered a grind. In fact, he wasn't much of a student at all. In his yearbook the editors wrote of him, "Being naturally bright, Joe says he never did much preparation and came to Yale to get finesse, éclat, savoir faire and to help his father." His aim, quite simply, was "to become a magnate." He came to love Yale, as do so many of those who attend, and when my turn came, I went there, too.

While at Yale, my father was also smitten with Frances Wolff, who was to become his wife and my mother. They met before he entered Yale, at a dance. Mother had contracted polio when she was over thirteen years old, and walked with a limp as a result of the disease. She also did not have the full use of her right arm and leg. She had difficulty walking and getting in and out of chairs.

Frances had gone to the dance to please her mother, but she and my father got along very well indeed. They saw each other often when Joe Junior was at Yale, and they wanted to get married after he graduated. There were obstacles in the form of their families, both of which opposed the match. The

Wolffs were Sephardic Jews, who looked down on German Jews. They were related to Benjamin Cardozo, who would later become a U.S. Supreme Court justice, and to other distinguished figures. To them my father was a parvenu. For their part, Joe and Zillah weren't too pleased when told their son intended to marry a cripple, who besides was not particularly well endowed financially. In any case, marriage was out of the question until Joe Junior got his start in business and could afford to support a wife and family.

I don't think my dad ever considered a career in any field other than tobacco. Even as a child, he knew he would enter the family business. Likewise, Joe Senior had never thought his son would not join him at Cullman Brothers, but Joe Senior wanted to make sure my father had the right stuff for this field.

As a child, Joe Junior spent a great deal of time with his father at the Water Street offices. They would walk through the district where so many of the nation's cigars were rolled. Joe Junior would watch the Cuban and Spanish cigarmakers combining tobaccos, shaping the cigar and then, after wrapping the binder around the filler, encasing it in a single sheet or wrapper. Grandfather taught him about tobacco, showed him sheaves that came from his warehouses, and occasionally rolled a cigar to instruct Joe Junior how it was done. And he introduced his son to the other cigarmakers, so that by the time Joe Junior was ready for Yale he already knew a great many of his colleagues and competitors.

This kind of preparation served my father well for the rest of his life. The unique thing about Dad was that although he was a very small factor in the tobacco business he knew all the big people. They respected him for his knowledge of tobacco and for what he stood for: his character, his personality, and his remarkable integrity. In time he would train me in somewhat the same way he had been familiarized with the business.

As a result of his early training, Joe Junior was well prepared for the next step in his tobacco education. Grandfather must have thought long and hard about what his son would do upon graduation. Clearly he wanted him to be even more conversant with all aspects of the business, from the ground up. So he decided that his eager and ambitious son should start in the tobacco sub-basement. He was to work first as a laborer at a tobacco farm in Wisconsin that was serviced by one of Grandfather's warehouses, then in Cuba on a large tobacco plantation owned by a business associate, and finally in the Cullman Brothers warehouses in Wisconsin and Ohio. The future looked bright for Joe Junior, but the present wasn't so appealing.

Dad spent a year and a half working in the fields. His starting pay was $12 a week. A dollar went quite far in those days, but this was hardly the kind of remuneration expected by a Yale graduate whose father ran a pretty profitable business. One day he received a wire telling him to return home. Joe Senior greeted him rather gruffly: "I just wanted to see if you could support yourself." Then he told Joe Junior that he was to become a partner in Cullman Brothers.

Dad's uncle Jake, who had never been healthy, died soon after Dad became a partner, which meant that my father was pushed into a post of great responsibility while still learning the ins and outs of the business. In time he would become one of the best-informed and best-regarded individuals in the tobacco community. After World War I, when the management of the Chase Bank needed expertise to reorganize the American Sumatra Tobacco Company, they called upon my father for help.

All the while he continued to woo Frances Wolff. She finally gave in, and they were married in 1906. After a brief honeymoon they went house hunting, and found a place in Manhattan at 46 West Sixty-ninth Street. Grandfather Cullman made a present of it—to my mother, not my father, as an indication of the high regard in which he held her.

The house is still there, and it looks like something out of *Upstairs, Downstairs.* It is a four-story brownstone, with a very steep stoop in front. Mother hated that stoop—it was difficult for her to go up and down because of her being crippled—but Nan, my brothers, and I loved the place.

My parents had a very happy marriage. Dad was very solicitous of Mother. He urged her to exercise, fish, engage in simple sports. I sometimes think they bought the house so Mother would have to make a stretch at walking up the stairs.

When my parents moved into the Sixty-ninth Street house, their lives seemed close to perfect. Joe Junior was working away at Cullman Brothers, which was doing quite well, while Mother stayed at home. There were dinner parties, family gatherings, and in 1910 the birth of their first child, Frances Nathan Cullman, whom we all called Nan.

Nan grew up to be a very attractive young lady, a spirited, warmhearted person who would do anything for her younger brothers. Nan loved sports, loved people, and was very gregarious. Two mishaps significantly affected her life: Nan had sleeping sickness while in her teens, and was later involved in a major automobile accident.

In 1933, coming home from Albert Lasker's estate (Lasker was a family friend and head of Lord and Thomas advertising firm) in Chicago, she had a terrible head-on crash, which she was fortunate to survive. Nan was never quite the same after that; she became more nervous, though no less warmhearted. Her first marriage, to an architect named Bob Jacobs, didn't work out over time. Her second husband was a very nice guy named Percy Boas. She had three children with Bob Jacobs and lived near us on the family compound in Stamford, Connecticut, acquired by my father in 1922, and we had a great relationship. Nan died in April 1993.

My brother Arthur was two years younger than I. We went to the same schools, and had fun together at Yale. After graduation he got a job at a company called Philip Morris through our dad, who was chummy with its chairman, Alfred Lyon. PM was the smallest cigarette company in those days. In 1942, when Cullman Brothers acquired control of Benson & Hedges, Arthur joined my father there.

His relationship with Dad was complex; in 1945, Arthur suffered a nervous breakdown. By then he was married to the former Cee Stein and they had four children. He left New York in 1946 and enrolled in the Ph.D. program at Ohio State University in Columbus, Ohio, where he became one of the most respected marketing professors. Among his students was Les Wexner, who later became head of The Limited Company. Les always tells people what a brilliant teacher Arthur was. Arthur died in 1992.

Edgar, who came next, is six years younger than I. He married Louise Bloomingdale in 1938. He has always loved the tobacco trade, and worked with Dad in tobacco when we bought control of Benson & Hedges. The two of them used to have intense arguments about the business. Edgar remained with the family business, and today is chairman of Culbro and General Cigar. We were always very close, and still are. It wasn't only business—the two of us, after all, are both wedded to tobacco; we also share other interests. We both love salmon and trout fishing, play tennis and golf, and we both served on the board of Hotchkiss School and have homes close to each other in Montego Bay, Jamaica.

Finally, there is Lewis, attractive and bright. We got along very well, and we still play tennis together. In the Navy in World War II, he became a meteorologist and served in North Africa. After he was discharged, Lewis opened his own business, becoming one of the first people to do a leveraged buyout. This was before Kohlberg, Kravis, Roberts got into that field. His first big deal was the sale of Orkin Exterminator, to Rollins Broadcasting. Lewis got a bundle of stock in Rollins as a fee, and that got him thinking about other deals. Today, he heads Cullman Ventures, which owns the At a Glance Group, a major maker of calendars and address books. Lewis is a significant philanthropist, and is married to Dorothy Cullman.

We were a great big happy family. Joe Junior—known as "Mr. Junior" in tobacco circles—was busy with his work, but remained an avid sportsman; he introduced us all to fishing, golf, tennis, football, and other sports. Like Joe Senior, he loved the opera and in season would go once a week to the old Met. Mother was super. She was very outspoken and not at all shy about standing up to Dad. She was a very positive force in all our lives, loving and gentle, and a very active person around the house. She liked to have those large family meals, so I saw my grandparents, uncles, aunts, and cousins quite often. Both my parents had a sense of family identity, and set for themselves strong ethical and moral standards, which they inculcated into their children. I suppose Mother was a more distinct influence on me when I was growing up than Dad, but that was quite natural in those days.

My brother Lewis recalls that when the time came for us boys to be told "the facts of life," it was Mother, not Father, who did the job. When Arthur's turn came Mother took out this book and started reading it to him. At one point, the book said, "Now ask him if he has any questions." So Mother did, and Arthur replied, "Yes. I always wondered how they manufactured paper."

I know it is fashionable nowadays to complain about family problems. We had some of these, to be sure, but the pluses far outnumbered the minuses.

As the family grew, the Sixty-ninth Street brownstone, which once seemed so huge to the newlyweds rattling around in it, became somewhat cramped. It had a basement for storage and deliveries. The kitchen was in the basement too, and the food was sent upstairs by means of a dumbwaiter. The icebox was there, along with a coal burning furnace which provided heat in the winters and hot water all year around. There was also a little sitting room next to the kitchen, where the help ate. We always had a cook and at least one woman whose primary job was to serve the meals. On the first floor there was a formal parlor, because my parents entertained frequently and needed a lot of space for all the people who came to their dinners and parties. There was a pantry behind the dining room, where the serving woman worked.

My parents' bedroom was on the second floor, along with a dressing room, a sitting room, and a bathroom. On the third floor was a big front bedroom for my brothers Arthur, Edgar, and Lewis, which they shared with Jules Neidle, who was a sort of combination tutor and companion.

Jules was a student at Columbia Law School; he received room and board and a small stipend for taking care of the Cullman children. Such arrangements were quite common in those days. If a family had many girls, they had a governess. There were four Cullman boys in addition to my sister, so we had Jules.

And way back on the third floor, facing the rear, was my very small bedroom. It was attached to a bathroom, over my father's bathroom.

On the fourth floor was Nan's room, and the room right next to that was occupied by my mother's maid, a woman named Mary Dolan. There were three other rooms: one for the other maid, one for the waitress, and one for a woman who helped out in the kitchen. We played stoop baseball on the steps leading to the entrance. Johnny Wolf, my closest friend for seventy-five years, lived at 49 West Sixty-ninth Street, Phoebe Hochstader Stein at 51 West Sixty-ninth.

Nancy and Michael Cardozo lived with our grandmother "Granny Wolff" at number 33. It was a friendly family street. I played ball in Central Park and went sleigh riding nearby. Joe Senior and my grandmother lived at 39 West Seventy-first Street. We saw them for Sunday lunches and on holidays, but not much more than that.

Years ago my mother had a town car, a Pierce Arrow. Later, when Mr. Junior felt affluent and wanted to give her something nice, he bought her a blue Rolls-Royce. This was during the Great Depression! Mother hated it. She had a terrible time getting in and out of the car, but she had a chauffeur, Charles Heiser, to drive and maintain it.

In 1922 Dad purchased a home in Stamford, Connecticut, from an attorney named Mike Goldsmith, a good friend of Dad's who had lost a great deal of money during the stock market collapse in 1921 and had a nervous breakdown. He told my father, "I have this large place in the country, and it's bothering me." Dad said, "I'll take it off your hands, sight unseen"—and he did, for $25,000. Then he told Mother about it. She wasn't too pleased at first. It was a two-and-a-half-hour drive from New York City, and that was the first thing that annoyed her about the place. Then they drove up a dirt road to the rustic house, in the middle of the wooded property, and all the while Mother was saying, "I'm not going to stay in the woods in a place like this. It's mosquito-infested and primitive."

She didn't care for the house either, which wasn't much more than a large log cabin. At the time it needed a generator to produce electricity and an artesian well for water. It wasn't the kind of place a person like my mother would like right away. But she soon changed her mind. The Far Rockaway house was sold, and we started spending more time at Cedar Lodge in Connecticut and adding to the house. This place was a most important part of my youth, a rustic rambling building on 150 acres. Cedar Lodge was also the summer home of my first cousins Nancy and Michael Cardozo, the children of my mother's sister Emily, who died of tuberculosis when my cousins were four and two years old. So it was a big summer family of seven children, and sister Nan was nine years older than my younger brother Lewis. Lots of summers, our tutor Jules Neidle came along. He became almost a part of our family.

Family times at Cedar Lodge were memorable because of the uniqueness of the place, its privacy and remoteness, the opportunities for horseback riding and tennis with Dad, sister Nan, and Edgar, the fun times the family enjoyed, and the extended use of the natural-looking swimming pool that Mother's brother John built. My parents would throw spectacular parties there, which many of the leading figures in the tobacco industry attended. Sister Nan's wedding to Robert Allan Jacobs took place at Cedar Lodge and the ushers, of whom I was one, wore high beaver hats for the ceremony.

My grandparents made us a present of a swimming pool in a shape that resembled the African continent, and Mother learned to swim, the exercise doing her a lot of good. Later, in 1942, Edgar rebuilt a house on the edge of the property. When my parents died, he purchased the entire Stamford property from their estate, and today he lives there with his wife Louise, as do Ellie and Edgar Cullman Jr. in the restored Cedar Lodge.

I have gone into all this to indicate that we lived well indeed. We made the move to New York in the 1920s, and continued living this way during the Great Depression period of the 1930s. From these descriptions one might easily assume the Cullmans were wealthy. We certainly were better off than the majority of Americans of the time, but we were not really rich. Rather, this is the way my dad wanted it to be. He earned a very good living but spent much of it on the living.

My parents, Joseph F. Cullman Jr. and Frances Wolff Cullman, at the party celebrating their forty-fifth wedding anniversary in 1953.

In my first sailor suit, 1918.

Rollerblading even then, 1923.

With tobacco distributor Burr Lichty, Waterloo, Iowa, 1932.

The Cullman family in the early 1930s. *Top row, left to right:* Joseph F. Cullman 3rd, Joseph Cullman Sr., Joseph F. Cullman Jr., Arthur Cullman. *Seated:* Edgar Cullman, Nan Cullman, Zillah Cullman (Mrs. Joseph Cullman Sr.), Frances Wolff Cullman, and Lewis Cullman.

The three Joes: Joseph F. Cullman 3rd, Joseph F. Cullman Sr., and Joseph F. Cullman Jr.

Susan Lehman Cullman and I at our wedding in Honolulu, 1935.

With man's best friends, my cocker spaniels, Cardi and Sherry, in the 1950s.

En route to the Los Angeles Olympics, 1932, with my friend Johnny Wolf.

Here I am with my daughter Dorothy
Cullman Treisman . . .

My brother Edgar and I when you
could keep a salmon.

and with her children, Joel and Jeffrey Treisman, my grandsons.

With my wife Joan at our first wedding, in 1974, with her children, Tracy and Barney.

Linda Hart with Joan and me, relaxing in East Hampton.

Lucky again! Tryall, Jamaica, 1991.

Three generations of Cullmans. *From left to right:* Lewis, Arthur, Nan, myself, and Edgar. In the portraits are our dad ("Mister Junior") and our grandfather, Joseph Senior.

I don't know what his financial situation was, but do recall that there were times when he was concerned about money, and there was talk of having to cut back and perhaps live in a smaller place. Grandfather had purchased some land in Simsbury, Connecticut, in 1910 on which we later grew leaf tobacco for cigar wrappers. Dad added to the land holdings with borrowed money—during the Depression interest was at a rate of less than 2 percent—and then sold what amounted to a futures contract for the leaf.

Dad was prone to worry about the price of tobacco, the weather, and the many other factors that affected growers of leaf tobacco. I suspect this was one of the reasons behind Dad's dark moods, which hit him every once in a while, and the depressions into which he would fall. He did have a couple of nervous breakdowns, and had to go to Bill Brown's sanitarium in Garrison, New York, in the late 1920s and early 1930s.

Another few words about Jules Neidle are in order, because of the important part he played in my life. He was a wonderful young man—friendly, attractive, intelligent. He appeared on the scene when I was about sixteen and away at school. My brothers were too young to drive. He would take them around and was more like an older brother than anything else.

Jules had a great sense of humor and decency. In those days no one talked about "role models," but that was what he was for us. All the children were fond of him. But one day my mother decided to tell him to leave us, not because there was an argument but because most of us were out of the house and she felt it was time he got married. And he did marry Catherine Strasburger in the mid-1930s, and had a legal career. We always kept in close touch, however, and he was never out of my life until his early death.

To return to my life on West Sixty-ninth Street: I made many friends in the neighborhood. We would roam Central

Park the way Dad did when he was a boy, and we played stoopball and a lot of other street games kids did then and I suppose still do today. Occasionally one of my brothers or I would go with Dad to the tobacco farms near Simsbury, so we had a good idea of how he made his living. I just assumed one day we would enter the business, as Dad had entered *his* father's. But it didn't turn out that way for all of us.

As I've mentioned, when I was a youngster I was enrolled in Ethical Culture School. I was quite content there, but one day my father took me aside and told me I was going to leave Ethical Culture and go to Hotchkiss instead. I wondered why. After all, I was doing well at Ethical Culture, and my parents belonged to the Society. One would think they would want me to stay there. But Dad was a dedicated Yale alumnus. He attended every Yale football game from the day he graduated in 1904 to his end. He wanted his firstborn son to follow in his footsteps at Yale.

For that matter, he wanted all of us to go to Yale. Quite typically, he told us that we could go to any college we wanted to, "but I'll pay your way through Yale." Hotchkiss was well-known as a feeder school for Yale. Boys who graduated from Hotchkiss normally got into Yale easily.

I didn't think to object. In those days, sons didn't argue about such matters, they simply did what their parents told them to do.

About a month before I was supposed to take my entrance examination for Hotchkiss, Dad took me aside again and asked, "How is your Latin, son?" "I don't know any Latin, Dad," I replied, and he said, "You'll have to take an examination in Latin soon, so you'd better learn and you don't have much time." So he got me a Latin tutor, a very nice lady, but I didn't seem to like Latin as much then as I did later. So, while she was supposed to be giving me lessons, I would be outside playing stoopball.

Needless to say, I didn't perform well on the Hotchkiss Latin exam, which was an important part of the entrance ritual. When the marks were released, we learned I had received a 50 in math, a like grade in English, and a 15 in Latin. Dad exploded. He was really angry—not primarily at me, but more at the school, which he felt had no right to give a son of his such grades. "They can't do that to us," he roared, pulling himself up to his full five-foot-six-inch height. "I'm going to go up there and see that man."

"That man" was George Van Santvoord, the revered headmaster of Hotchkiss. So we drove two hours to Hotchkiss, which was an impressive-looking place in Lakeville, Connecticut, in the hilly, green, northwestern part of the state. The school had about a half-dozen buildings at the time, the main one a beautiful colonial style. We parked the car and swept into Mr. Van Santvoord's offices. The headmaster was six feet four inches tall, and he looked and sounded like what I imagined God would be like had He decided to come to earth in rural Connecticut. At that moment I felt pretty insignificant.

By then Dad had cooled down considerably. All his life he had dealt with clever people, selling, working out deals, and now he would try his skills on the headmaster. "I don't understand this, Mr. Van Santvoord. Here is my son, who bears my name and who I know is very bright and earnest. And he has been rejected by Hotchkiss. Can you tell me why this is so?"

Mr. Van Santvoord was unusually decent and polite, and he handled my father very well. He had been through scenes like this many times. He looked Dad in the eye, smiled benevolently, and simply said, "Let's look at the exams." So down came the blue books, every one of which had red slashes on almost every page. By the time Mr. Van Santvoord finished going over them, Dad knew he was licked. His dreams of my attending Yale must have seemed quite remote.

Mr. Van Santvoord wasn't finished. There was hope, and

he threw out the academic lifeline to the Cullmans. "Your son just isn't scholastically ready for Hotchkiss." I was a little guy, small for my age, and he might have thought me younger than I actually was. A short spell polishing me up would do no harm, and might do the trick. "Why don't you send Joe here to the Fessenden School?" I don't think my Dad ever heard of Fessenden, which was a feeder for Hotchkiss just as Hotchkiss was a feeder for Yale. It turned out that Mr. Van Santvoord had sent quite a few boys to Fessenden for the same reason he was recommending I go there. Dad now realized all could turn out well after all.

So I went to Fessenden, which was in West Newton, Massachusetts, just outside Boston. One got there from New York by taking the New Haven Railroad to Boston and then a streetcar to the school. It was a rather small place, with three or four buildings, and it was a pre-prep for top secondary schools. I have a good recollection of Fessenden; I got good marks and entered Hotchkiss easily.

Many years later I read Louis Auchincloss' novel *The Rector of Justin,* which may have been influenced by the author's experiences at Groton, a place I suspect wasn't much different from Hotchkiss. Those who have not attended a school like Hotchkiss or Groton can get an idea of what such places are like from that book. The boys at Hotchkiss called George Van Santvoord "the Duke." All the boys respected Mr. Van Santvoord, who was more than a little terrifying. I think he led the school well. Hotchkiss had a practice of letting boys who received an average of more than 70 in a course skip the final term exams. As a result they were able to go home a few days earlier. I managed to skip most of the exams, and went home early many times, but every report Mr. Van Santvoord sent home read, "Good, but should do much better." He was a most demanding person, but a great scholar.

Hotchkiss provided me with an excellent education. The

courses were demanding, the students bright and hardworking, the masters outstanding, and the curriculum carefully worked out. You really had to work to meet the high standards. That's just what I did, and in addition I participated in sports, was handball champion, and was business manager of the *Hotchkiss Record*, the school newspaper. I made some great friends, such as James Linen, who became CEO of Time Inc.

The school had an organized chapel and regular vespers services which I attended. At the time I did not feel that this was in conflict with my Jewish heritage. In fact, I rather enjoyed the services. Perhaps I had been prepared for them by my attendance at Ethical Culture School. I can understand why some people protest religious services in schools, but on a purely personal level they weren't a problem for me. I came to consider the services as part of my education, and vespers a time for reflection and contemplation.

As I said, Lakeville, Connecticut, was a lovely, bucolic place, and the school had an outstanding faculty. Classes were small—maybe fifteen or twenty students—and there was plenty of opportunity for discussion. My history teacher was "Pop" Jefferson, who was very dramatic. I can remember part of one lecture dealing with a seventeenth-century war between France and Spain. Jefferson went over the battles, and why France won, marking her domination over Spain. He ended with a rhetorical flourish: "Poof, the Pyrenees are no more!" Strange what you remember. That was seventy years ago, after all.

I had other marvelous teachers. Hick Williams in Latin, which I was finally learning. "Howdy" Edgar introduced me to the classics of English literature—Thomas Hardy, Charles Dickens, John Galsworthy, Jane Austen, and Anthony Trollope. Carl Parsons was another fine English teacher. I took his course on Shakespeare, which I found most enjoyable and edifying. At Hotchkiss I came to realize that a learned person with the gift for analysis and discussion can become an extraordinary teacher. I started to wonder whether I had it in me to become such a person.

As much as I enjoyed literature, however, my real love was history: in time I focused on military history, and naval history in particular. Under different circumstances, I might have wound up on a college faculty, leading the kind of life my brother Arthur had. But there was the family business to consider. I was the oldest son, and in the European tradition my family still retained, that meant I was destined to follow Dad's career in tobacco at Cullman Brothers.

The students at Hotchkiss were attractive—from all over the United States; many entered Yale in the same class as I did. I roomed the last three years at Yale with a Hotchkiss friend, George Elmore from Washington, Connecticut.

I still see a few old grads at Hotchkiss reunions, which I attend whenever I can. I remember George Atterbury, whose father, William, headed the Pennsylvania Railroad, at the time one of the premier American corporations. And, as I said, I liked and admired Jim Linen, who became the CEO at Time and chairman of the Hotchkiss board, and Bill Mc-Knight, who was a very prominent partner at Breed, Abbott & Morgan.

I spent vacations at home, traveling by bus from Hotchkiss to Millerton, and then by train—the New York Central—to Grand Central Station. The trip took three hours, and went through countryside that in those days was rural but today is developed. But there weren't many vacations. I arrived at Hotchkiss in mid-September and didn't come home until mid-December.

It was a damned good experience for me. It significantly changed my life. I grew up a lot. I took a bit of kicking around. I graduated and was accepted at Yale as a member of the class of 1935. I later served on the Hotchkiss board. I took a gorgeous girl from the Bennett School in Milbrook, New York, to the Hotchkiss senior prom. Her name was Veronica Balfe. I liked her, but shortly after I graduated she married Gary Cooper.

I might add here that Dad was pleased with the way things worked out for me. As a result, my brothers also took the Fessenden-Hotchkiss-Yale route.

Meanwhile, Cullman Brothers was doing well, encouraging Dad to seek other ways to channel his energies. Early in 1929 he organized a closed-end investment trust called Tobacco and Allied Stocks, Incorporated. Listed on what was then called the New York Curb Exchange, it was the first investment trust to specialize in a single industry, tobacco. In effect, my father, who knew the industry as well as anyone, was offering to use his brains and knowledge for the benefit of other investors, who purchased shares.

Tobacco and Allied was a small affair, capitalized at only $3 million. The Cullmans took 10 percent of the shares and received warrants that enabled us, over time, to increase our holdings to 40 percent. Tobacco and Allied also differed from most other investment trusts at that time in that it was not highly leveraged and not meant to be a speculative vehicle. Rather, the public was told that the company's policy would be to offer investors a chance to capitalize on the thinking of Dad, Howard, and other individuals who were deeply involved in the tobacco industry and knew the companies in which they invested very well. The largest positions Tobacco and Allied had were in such familiar companies as American Tobacco, R. J. Reynolds, Imperial Tobacco, and Philip Morris.

The management of Tobacco and Allied didn't require much time. The portfolio was not traded very actively, and virtually all the dividends received from the companies in the portfolio were paid out to shareholders. To all involved it seemed to be a nice, small operation. Of course, we couldn't imagine how this small investment trust would alter the lives of all the Cullman family.

The second major business event of 1929 for Cullman Brothers was the firm's entry into cigar manufacturing proper. Until then the company had been a grower and a broker, but that year officials at Chase National Bank, who had been impressed with the way Dad had reorganized American Sumatra, asked him to run a small cigar company—Webster-Eisenlohr—which was in deep trouble. In fact, its problems reportedly had helped induce the previous president of Webster to commit suicide. Chase Bank, which had taken Webster-Eisenlohr stock as collateral for a loan, now owned the stock and controlled the company.

The Chase people weren't interested in getting into the cigar business. All they wanted to do was to get their money out of the business. But to do this they would first have to find someone to whip Webster into decent shape. So Chase offered Dad a large block of preferred stock at the knock-down price of $40 a share if he would take over. He did, and so became a small factor in the cigar business as well as in leaf tobacco. My father managed the company, but Chase continued to own a controlling interest.

Webster had factories in Harrisburg and York, Pennsylvania, and toward the end of the decade had sales of between $30 million and $40 million a year. It turned out a brand called Cinco—Spanish for "Five"—that cost a nickel. Webster was the premium brand name. The Webster Golden Wedding brand was a dime; Webster Queens were two for twenty-five cents, and Webster Fancy Tails fifteen cents. This group of Webster brands hadn't done too well under the old management, but we changed the packaging and the blend and we made Webster the number one high-grade cigar in America, outselling the old leader, Robert Burns.

DAD FIRST GOT INTO THE CIGARETTE business in 1942. While on a fishing trip in a remote part of northeastern Canada, he received a phone call from Richmond, Virginia. The connection was bad, and my father had had some drinks. So after a few minutes of unintelligible talk he shouted "Yes!" into the receiver and slammed it down. When he returned home, he learned that he had unwittingly purchased an interest in a small, very old cigarette company called Axton-Fisher, which had three main brands: Twenty Grand, Fleetwood, and Spud. Spud was the first of the mentholated cigarettes. Altogether Axton-Fisher had less than one percent of the cigarette market.

Axton-Fisher was controlled by the Bank of America, then headed by founder A. P. Giannini. When World War II started, the price of cigarette tobacco went through the roof, and Dad wanted to liquidate the company by selling off its inventory of more than 25 million pounds of tobacco, a move that would have benefited the stockholders. Giannini refused to go along, so Dad sold his stock to the Bank of America in 1943. Six months later Giannini sold the tobacco and the rest of the company to Philip Morris, just as Dad had suggested, whereupon the former stockholders, including my father, sued. The case dragged on, but in the end the stockholders won and were paid off.

Meanwhile, in 1931, I was off to college. Yale was a big challenge to me mentally and physically. I majored in history and Charles Seymour, who taught modern history, was the most influential teacher I met. Seymour was not only a fine lecturer, but also an exciting, inspiring man, warm and engaging, who could spice his recitations with personal experiences. When he talked about the Treaty of Versailles, it was as one who'd been part of the American mission advising President Wilson. Later on Seymour became president of Yale.

Clare Mendel, a 1904 classmate of Dad's, and dean while I was there, also offered a course in modern history. As I have said, I have always been interested in naval history, so when the time came for me to write my senior thesis, I selected the Battle of Jutland in 1916, an indecisive struggle between the British and German fleets. This same interest led me to join Naval ROTC in my sophomore year. In those days, NROTC was an extra course. You drilled twice a month and took classes in naval seamanship, gunnery, and tactics; also required was an NROTC cruise, which I took on the USS *Overton* as a seaman second class. The *Overton* was a four-stack coal-burning destroyer from World War I. Naval appropriations were then very low, and I can remember thinking that if we had to go to war with equipment like this, our chances of winning wouldn't be very good. But I didn't take the Navy seriously. I never considered a naval career, and didn't believe in 1934 I would be called to active duty. As it turned out, taking NROTC proved one of the most important early decisions of my life.

I made many friends at Yale, and I still keep in contact with some of them. I participated actively in athletics. For many men in those days, going to college meant trying out for one team or another. At Hotchkiss I had participated in several sports, and was the school handball champion and runner-up in the golf championship. I was a little guy, weighing around 135 pounds, but I went out for football anyway. I made the freshman and junior varsity squad at Yale and played on the 150-pound football team. I wouldn't try it now, given the size of today's players, but football players were smaller in the 1930s. I also played lots of squash and tennis.

I tried to earn a place for myself on the *Yale Daily News*, and for a little while I thought I had made the grade there.

One day, the managing director, James Quig Newton, who went on to become the mayor of Denver, dropped by my room and said, "Joe, congratulations. You have been elected to the *News*." That was a thrill, something I wanted badly. I telephoned Dad to let him know, telling him it would be announced the next day. But when the release was made public, I ended up in sixth place, and the *News* would only take five.

I don't tell this story for the reason you might suspect. At the time, many people said my rejection was obviously the result of anti-Semitism. But there were other factors at work, like campus politics. Some of those who came out ahead of me had connections with various fraternities, but at that time I hadn't joined one of them, although I later was elected to Zeta Psi, which was Dad's fraternity too. I never concealed my religion. I have always been proud to be Jewish. People knew I was Jewish, and yes, I was invited to lots of social gatherings while at Hotchkiss and Yale, and had a great deal of fun.

During the summers I worked for my father as a cigar missionary, one of the toughest jobs he could find for me. He wanted me to get in at the bottom and work my way up. That's what Joe Senior had done for him, and now he was giving me a taste of what he felt I had to do. I didn't mind it, and realized this was a good way to learn the business from the ground up.

I would travel around New York City in a panel truck with boxes of various Webster-Eisenlohr cigars, making cold calls on neighborhood cigar stores. I would walk in, go to the proprietor, and say, "I'm Joe Cullman and I'm selling Webster and Girard cigars," and then go into a pitch. It was tough sledding, and I quickly learned to handle rejection. If I got an order at all, it might be for 100 or so cigars. I would go back to the truck, get the cigars, bring them into the store, and place them in the display case. A few weeks later I would return to see how things were going. If I was fortunate, most of the cigars would be sold, and I would take a new order. Most of the time I wasn't that fortunate: this was during the Great Depression, and men who used to smoke twenty-five-cent cigars were buying dime and nickel brands, while those who had smoked five nickel cigars a day during the good years were down to one or two.

The whole country had problems in this period, and mine were minor compared to what I was hearing and seeing. I had entered Yale in 1931, when the unemployment rate was 16 percent and not getting any better. By 1933, it had risen to almost 25 percent. It is sometimes difficult to get people who did not live through those years to appreciate what these numbers meant. In a period when most families had a single bread-winner, one family in four had no wages upon which to rely. It was a staggering statistic.

Whenever I went home, I would see Dad looking like a beaten man. His fits of depression came more often and lasted longer. As for my personal situation, I had taken the rejection by the *News* far too seriously. It affected my grades, and for a while I thought I might leave Yale. So between the hard times at Cullman Brothers and Yale, it looked as though one way or the other I would be leaving New Haven to get a job in the worst labor market in American history.

Between the missionary work and conditions in the family business, I was learning something about life that wasn't taught at Hotchkiss or Yale. The people to whom I was trying to sell cigars looked upon me as beneath them. If they took a box or two of cigars, they thought they were doing me a favor—well, if the truth be told, they were. The tobacco business puts one in touch with a million or more retailers in the United States. Of course, I called on relatively few of them, but through them I learned how difficult it was to get by in the United States in that period. I don't think that individuals who worked in the so-called privileged world of the time, where many of my classmates wound up, appreciated this as much as I did.

Newsreels of the time seem to concentrate on men in business suits selling apples on street corners. I saw them quite often as I made my rounds, going from rejection to rejection. I saw men and women near the back doors of restaurants, picking through the garbage for food. It bothered me then, and I think of it now whenever I see homeless people in New York.

As it turned out, none of my fears was realized. Dad's business suffered, but was never in danger of collapse, and my grades picked up. I graduated with my class in 1935. My parents were there for the ceremony, after which my father said it was one of the proudest days of his life—not so much because I graduated from his alma mater, but because of my commission as an ensign in the Naval Reserve.

Shortly after graduation, on August 2, 1935, I married Susan Lehman, whom I had met two years earlier when she was a student at Vassar. Susan was very bright, tall, and beautiful. She was a real charmer, who loved the outdoors and was a good athlete. We shared many interests. No wonder, then, that I was immediately attracted to her. We saw each other as much as possible, and became engaged during my senior year.

Susan's mother, Cecile, had a beautiful estate called Willowpond, on the Hudson at Tarrytown, New York. We had a large engagement party there and were to be married there in the fall, but that was not to be.

Cecile had planned a trip in summer 1935 to Hawaii with her daughters Sue and Betty; engagement or no engagement, she insisted on going, so I asked if I could come along. Cecile said yes but didn't realize that we would ask her to let us marry out there. She agreed, and Sue and I were married at the Royal Hawaiian Hotel on August 2, 1935. Only my old friend Ardie Deutsch and the Yale baseball team attended. They called the Royal Hawaiian the Pink Palace; it was gorgeous.

We spent our first married night at the Halakalani next door, flew to the island of Kauai for a brief honeymoon, and then took the SS *Lurline* to San Francisco, where we went to a big party with Wally Haas, Jr. (Wally later asked me to be the first outside director of Levi Strauss). We then motored across the United States in the family Buick. Back in New York City, we took an apartment at 50 East Seventy-seventh Street and I started work at Schulte's. Two years later we purchased a house on Sleepy Hollow Road in Briarcliff Manor, New York. We bought the place from Eleanor and Franklin Roosevelt's daughter, Cissie Dahl.

The economy was still in bad shape in 1935, but the situation was improving, if you can call a 20 percent unemployment rate an improvement. The Works Progress Administration swung into operation about the time I graduated, the Rural Electrification Administration opened for business, and the law establishing Social Security was signed by the President. My father, who had helped draft the National Recovery Administration's tobacco code, marched in NRA parades before the Supreme Court eventually declared the National Recovery Administration unconstitutional. He had become a staunch Democrat, and would become angry if anyone had a harsh word to say about FDR.

I don't think many Americans would have called the outlook for the country and the world hopeful. Hitler and Mussolini were in power in Germany and Italy, while Stalin ruled in the USSR. Japan had invaded China. The chances of war were high, but this time it seemed the United States might remain neutral—or at least, that was the hope of many of us. And there I was, a chip on the surface of American life. I remember being troubled by it all.

# CHAPTER TWO

# From Cigar-Store Clerk to Naval Officer

*I wish I could tell you about the South Pacific. The way it actually was. The endless ocean. The infinite specks of coral we called islands. Coconut palms nodding gracefully toward the ocean. Reefs upon which waves broke into spray, and inner lagoons, lovely beyond description. I wish I could tell you about the sweating jungle, the full moon rising behind the volcanoes, and the waiting. The waiting. The timeless, repetitive waiting.*

—James A. Michener
*TALES OF THE SOUTH PACIFIC*

IN 1935 I WAS A YALE GRADUATE and married. I had a father who was a firm believer in two things about my career. First, as his oldest son I was in line to inherit leadership of Cullman Brothers; that prospect was pleasant for me if not so pleasant for my siblings. The second part of Dad's rock-solid creed was that people should start at the bottom. I had already undergone my training as a missionary man for Webster cigars during the summer recesses. Now I was given the chance to see what it was like on the other side of the transaction. I was to be a cigar-store clerk.

Dad used pull to get me the job. Webster sold cigars to many of the city's cigar stores, and one of the biggest chains was Schulte's. In 1935 the New York business districts were dotted with these cigar stores, where a person could also get other forms of tobacco as well as candy and other items. Dad got in touch with the head buyer at Schulte's; I was interviewed and got a job at Schulte's at 29 New Street, not far from the New York Stock Exchange.

I worked six days a week, ten hours a day, for which I received $15 a week, out of which were taken my union dues. I don't remember having any trouble with those long hours, but I liked to listen to radio broadcasts of the Yale football games. When I was on the job, it was against the rules to listen to the radio, so on Saturdays I would telephone home and Sue would put the radio on for me to listen to the game by phone.

I must confess that I didn't look forward to that first day on the job. I had learned that recently the store had been robbed and the manager shoved into the toilet. It was a dangerous job. We had money in the till; times were bad, and the temptation to burglarize was there.

I accepted the work, but at first felt out of place. Yale men weren't supposed to work as cigar-store clerks, even during the Depression, and Dad could have used me at Cullman Brothers. But in retrospect I have to say that it was a good experience: I learned how to sell.

If a customer came in and asked for a pack of Chesterfields, you were supposed to hand it to him while asking whether he needed razor blades or some other product in stock. If you failed to do this, and the manager found out, you would be reprimanded the first time, and perhaps fired if it happened often again. The manager knew there were plenty of others out there who would be delighted to clerk for $15 a week.

I came to realize how a business operated, how to motivate workers, how to talk with them, how to joke with customers in ways that would lead to repeat business. We had our regular customers, people who worked in the area, and I tried to remember their names, facts about their families and the companies for which they worked, what brands of cigars and cigarettes they bought, which brand of gum they chewed, and much more.

My stay at Schulte's was not very long. I started in early autumn of 1935 and was there until January 1936, when Dad told me that it was time for the next chapter of my post-Yale education. At a similar stage in his life, Grandfather had sent him to Cuba, and now I was to go there to learn about the care and cultivation of cigar tobacco leaf and how to manufacture Cuban cigars.

As he had with Schulte's, Dad got me the job. Webster imported a good deal of Cuban tobacco, part of the blend for its cigars, which had a Wisconsin binder and a Connecticut-grown shade leaf wrapper over a Cuban filler. All that for a ten-cent Webster Golden Wedding. Dad arranged for me to work with the people at H. Uppmann in Havana, one of the finest names in cigars. So I was to learn from the best in the business.

Before I left, Dad took me aside and gave me my marching orders. I was to learn all I could about making quality cigars. Naturally, being his son and having listened to his stories for all those years I already knew quite a bit, but now I had to learn still more. I was to be a sort of apprentice tobacco blender and cigarmaker. I already knew the theory. Now would come the practice.

Sue and I spent half a year in Havana. I worked hard, but Sue and I also enjoyed ourselves. We rented a little house outside Havana on the grounds of the Country Club where Johnny Farrell, U.S. Open Champion in 1928, was the pro; Sue and I had a second honeymoon in what for us was an exotic spot. I loved to go to the racetrack at Oriental Park. At that time Havana was a great place for young, well-to-do Americans—it was lively and very cosmopolitan—but it was also very corrupt. The dictator Fulgencio Batista was in power, where he would remain until ousted by Fidel Castro in 1959.

It was in Havana that I first met Ernest Hemingway. I wouldn't say I palled around with him, but we did have some conversations. Hemingway was someone whose works I had enjoyed while in college and later, and whose fascination with East Africa I would come to share. He hung around in a bistro and bar called the Floridita, and that was where we met and talked.

Sue and I returned home in the autumn of 1936. I had done what my father required of me. There is no university where a person can learn the cigar business. The subject wasn't and isn't taught in graduate schools of business, or even specialized academies. The only way to learn it is through an apprenticeship. I now had served three of them—as missionary man, sales clerk, and manufacturer.

I went to work for Webster-Eisenlohr, which was located at 187 Madison Avenue, between Thirty-fourth and Thirty-fifth Streets. My job was in promotion. We had several low-priced cigars, which in those days sold for five cents. Webster, at ten cents and up, was our centerpiece brand and my main responsibility.

Sue and I lived in Briarcliff and in our East Seventy-seventh Street apartment. In December 1939 our daughter Dorothy was born, and life was good, although reading the news and listening to the radio were worrisome. I remember the shock of hearing that the Germans had invaded Poland on September 1, 1939, and that England and France had declared war on Germany. At that moment I was driving to Lake Placid with Dick Dammann. I was on my way to compete in the Adirondack Amateur Golf Championship in match play, which I won.

The cigar business was quite complicated, more so than cigarettes. There were two large companies. Consolidated Cigar, which was formed in 1929 by, as the name indicates, consolidating several companies in an attempt to create an industry giant, was the leading manufacturer of medium- and low-priced cigars, such as El Producto, Harvester, Dutch Masters, La Palina, and Muriel. It grew much of its wrapper tobacco in Connecticut and Massachusetts, and purchased shade wrapper and binders from companies like Cullman Brothers. General Cigar, the other large company, made White Owl, Robert Burns, Van Dyck, and William Penn. Besides these two there were scores of much smaller, regional companies, of which Webster-Eisenlohr was one. Dad got a kick out of being a manufacturer, and wanted to make a go of it.

We had a very fine distributor called the Metropolitan Tobacco Company, which had around 200 salesmen in the greater New York area. Metropolitan distributed products sold in cigar and sundries stores. I was to go out with Metropolitan salesmen and perform missionary or promotion work. They operated mostly from panel trucks. We would go into a drugstore, a restaurant, a candy store, or a neighborhood stationery store. The Metropolitan salesman usually was known to the proprietor. They would make some small talk as I stood and watched. Then the salesman would take orders for cigarettes, sundries, and so on.

At the end of this he would turn to me and say, "And now I want you to meet Mr. Joseph Cullman from the Webster-Eisenlohr people. He would like a few minutes of your time to tell you about his line of cigars." I would go into my pitch, which usually ended with the proprietor saying he didn't want any of our cigars. It was an uphill battle, and I got thrown out of many places, but the Metropolitan people were quite helpful to me. They would give me a boost, which the proprietors sometimes would accept.

If the dealer bought 100 or 200 cigars, I would throw in some extras as a reward. Sometimes a tobacconist would ask me how much extra he would get. I might give him five cigars for an order of one hundred, and he might reply that that wasn't enough. If I made the deal I would then go back to the truck, bring in the cigars, and try to have them displayed prominently on the counter or on the case. So that was a start.

I worked on Webster sales from the autumn of 1936 until March 1941, when I went on active duty in the Navy. It was a good experience. I learned what rejection and success were like. Webster became the number one high-grade cigar in America by the mid-1940s. The company was doing well under Dad's leadership. He had put it solidly in the black, which should have pleased the Chase bank. But then a jealous senior officer accused him of a conflict of interest, claiming that he made Webster purchase its wrappers from Cullman Brothers. The officer persuaded Chase that Joe Cullman Jr. was not the proper person to run Webster-Eisenlohr, even though he had made it profitable. So they asked him to step down as CEO and take the post of chairman. Furious, Dad swore he would never be involved in a company he did not control.

After losing control of Webster, Dad was at loose ends. He had enjoyed working at the company, and now he had time on his hands. But not for long. Later in 1941 he became interested in Benson & Hedges, originally a U.K. firm, which in 1899 opened a retail store in New York. At the time Benson & Hedges was not a manufacturing operation, but rather imported cigarettes rolled in London, which were sold from a store in a brownstone at 288 Fifth Avenue. In time, however, B&H would import tobacco and paper and hand-roll the cigarettes in the shop. Then, when demand increased, the company opened a small factory farther downtown.

As activity in the city moved north, so did the store, first to 314 Fifth Avenue and then to a leased six-story building at 435 Fifth Avenue and Thirty-ninth Street, where Benson & Hedges operated a retail outlet on the ground floor and had an office, subleasing the rest of the building to tenants. There B&H was in 1941, when Dad started looking it over.

At the time the company was selling 95 million cigarettes a year, which actually made it one of the smallest in the industry. But even though B&H was profitable, management decided to explore the possibility of selling it, figuring that it should get a good price given the industry's growth. For a brief period Philip Morris, the smallest of the smaller major cigarette firms, considered a purchase. Like Benson & Hedges, Philip Morris had started out British; its product was viewed as an upscale smoke. The fit with B&H would have made sense, and for a while during the 1930s, PM executives actually bought into B&H as though in preparation for a takeover. But at that time the major cigarette companies were facing antitrust prosecution, and in the end PM didn't make the purchase.

Alfred Lyon, a Philip Morris executive who later would become involved with the Axton-Fisher purchase and was one of Dad's friends, told him about the situation. Dad looked it over and liked what he found; his interest prevailed. Tobacco and Allied purchased a 51 percent position in Benson & Hedges, at a cost of $850,000. This violated every rule in

Dad's personal book. He had vowed never to pay more than book value for a company, never to pay more than a certain price–earnings ratio, but he was attracted by this company, which T&A would control. After the Webster disappointment he wanted to make certain he would take orders from no one, and the Cullmans were major shareholders of T&A.

B&H was a jewel of a company: the American segment had an interesting history, which will explain what attracted Joe Junior to it. I go into some detail at this point, because while in 1941 it was small, B&H was to change all of our lives, mine in particular.

If, in this period, you could have walked through Benson & Hedges' small, elegant shop at 435 Fifth Avenue near Thirty-ninth Street, you might be forgiven for thinking you had entered a time warp and had been transported to Victorian London. The manager wore a morning coat, the staff knew most of the customers by name, and the interior looked more like an ornate, exclusive jewelry store than a tobacco shop. Until World War I the staff even served afternoon tea and cucumber sandwiches on inlaid teak tables to its upper-crust clientele. In those days a telephone order would bring cigarettes to anyone in the delivery area within fifteen minutes, carried by uniformed messenger boys. The company also sold high-priced cigars and pipe-tobacco mixes unavailable in other cigar stores like Schulte's. To accommodate its clients, B&H also operated small stores in Newport, Rhode Island, and Palm Beach, Florida, "in season."

This is to suggest that Benson & Hedges wasn't at all like the typical American cigarette company. The store had a distinguished customer base, mostly in the plush areas of Manhattan. One got the impression that the B&H people behind the counter might turn down a stranger coming through the door in search of a pack of their special cigarettes. Of course, this wasn't so, but the place was absolutely English.

B&H sold the Rolls-Royce of cigars. Its cigarettes, with all Virginia or Turkish leaf, were exotic to Americans accustomed to cigarettes made from blended bright and burley tobacco, and the cigars B&H sold started at around 65 cents, which made them comparable to today's $10 brands. B&H had fancy cigarettes: scented cigarettes with gold paper tips; handmade cigarettes with names like Old Gubek No. 11, available with plain, cork, or gold tips; a five-inch cigarette called Russian 5; a perfumed cigarette called Ambar, with gold tips; and Magnolia Rounds, also with gold tips. You get the idea. These were distinctive cigarettes, for those who not only wanted the best tobaccos and didn't care about price, but also wanted to be noticed. These were cigarettes that could only be purchased from B&H.

The company's factory was run by an extraordinarily able and imaginative man, Sidney Bach. Bach had gotten his hands on a special German cigarette-making machine that could turn out Russian-style cigarettes, with cardboard-filter mouthpieces. This unusual configuration was the kind of cigarette upper-class Europeans smoked after the British and French soldiers got them from Russians during the Crimean War. With his machine, Bach moved production to a factory on Water Street, in lower Manhattan near the East River, where approximately a hundred workers produced all the B&H brands.

Bach was convinced that the company's future rested with two new cigarettes he had introduced years earlier. One, with all Virginia tobacco, was Virginia Rounds; the other, with a filter mouthpiece, was Parliament. It was a bad time to come out with new brands. In 1930, unit sales in the United States had come close to 200 billion; they plunged to 113.5 billion in 1931. In such periods manufacturers tended to cut back or go to their economy brands. B&H, in contrast, was introducing premium products.

Virginia Rounds was an all-Virginia-tobacco cigarette

with an unusual corn tip. Virginia Rounds initially appeared in the same expensive package as other B&H brands. The brand did so well, perhaps because of its modest but effective advertising budget, that it was given a new, less expensive package and sold for the price of 25 cents for a package of twenty, which was a high price in those days.

Parliament was a blend of Virginia, burley, and Turkish tobaccos, and contained flavorings such as licorice, apple juice, and brown sugar. Smokers of lower-cost brands were rather surprised and often pleased by Parliaments, because they had never before experienced so smooth a smoke. Parliaments had a cardboard mouthpiece and a recessed cotton filter and came in costly cardboard slide and shell boxes. The filter was partly designed to reduce tar and nicotine, but mostly to keep bits of tobacco out of the smoker's mouth.

The cardboard mouthpieces were right out of the Russian nineteenth-century tradition, but the name indicated an English origin, probably for snob appeal. You might think the mouthpiece and filter and the box made the cigarettes more costly to produce, and they did—but the mouthpiece and cotton replaced tobacco, which was even more expensive. Al Lyon used to kid my father about this. "What do you care if tobacco prices go up? You can always beat that by giving Parliaments a longer mouthpiece."

It was the cardboard box that added significantly to manufacturing costs, and the cigarettes had to be packed into those boxes by hand. B&H couldn't change the package without losing sales. Indeed, that box was so popular and unique that in those days it wasn't unusual for a person to purchase one pack of Parliaments and then, when finished, buy his regular brand and place the cigarettes in the Parliament box, as a sort of cigarette case.

Parliament, more popular than Virginia Rounds, sold initially for 25 cents for twenty, but in 1932 the price was boosted to 30 cents, twice the price of ordinary smokes. It was the first blended cigarette with a filter that caught on with the American public. But there was a very limited following for Parliament, and at first it was not promoted; B&H was so small it couldn't afford advertisements for both Virginia Rounds and Parliament.

B&H's business expanded during the thirties; what the entire industry learned in this period is that smoking increases during economic depressions. Besides, the kind of person who was a regular B&H customer escaped most of the pain associated with bad times. I was told that the impresario E. F. Albee, the father of the playwright, sent boxes of cigars at Christmas to those on his gift list. The practice in this period was to run up a tab, and then pay once a year. Mr. Albee's tab was generally between $8,000 and $15,000. This was at a time when two-for-a-nickel cigars were very popular among the masses, and the 10- and 15-cent Websters were deemed a quality smoke.

This is the company Tobacco & Allied acquired in late 1941. My father was very much a hands-on manager. He was accustomed to dealing with small operations and did not like to delegate work. Why should he? He was a very good leaf man and manufacturing man, and he had strong ideas regarding promotion and advertising. He would have been out of place in a large organization. Webster-Eisenlohr was the right size for him, and so was B&H. He saw that the B&H store sold only high-grade products.

Now he could devote mornings to Cullman Brothers and afternoons to Benson & Hedges. He was a happy man. He used to sit on the balcony that overlooked the sales floor and watch what was happening. When a customer came in and purchased a box of dollar cigars, his face was wreathed in a smile. "Very nice," he murmured. In 1941 B&H reported sales of $2.1 million, and earned $158,000. Hardly a giant.

IN THE FALL OF 1942, after Dad had closed on the B&H purchase, I was in the Navy and about to ship out for overseas, leaving behind my wife and our two-year-old daughter, as well as everyone I knew. When Dad took over as CEO of Benson & Hedges in 1943, I was in the midst of the fighting on the U.S. cruiser *Montpelier* in the South Pacific around Guadalcanal. This was the next stage in my education, and in many respects the most important.

Until then most of the people I socialized with were of the same social and economic class as I. Now this was to change. I was thrown in with Americans from all parts of the nation, of all religions and classes; and, of course, the same was true for them. It was an important experience for me. I was to hold several very responsible positions after I left the Navy, but none of them was as important as the one I filled from 1941 to 1945.

I spent four and a half years in the Navy, most of that in a combat zone. Most of the men I served with in this period are now either dead or relying on Social Security. But in the recesses of my mind they remain young, as I was then. The experiences we shared were important to all of us, and so I would like to tell you about some of them, and what it was like to fight in the South Pacific during World War II. I thought readers might like this glimpse into what one writer called "the last good war."

I've already mentioned that I had been commissioned an ensign in the Naval Reserve in 1935. In March 1941, nine months before the United States entered World War II, I was called to active duty. The Battle of Britain was still on; Hitler's armies had already invaded Poland, Belgium, the Netherlands, Luxembourg, and France and were about to go deep into the Soviet Union. The outlook for the Allies was bleak. Just about everyone still hoped we wouldn't get into the war, but anyone with a sense of history and an awareness of the situation realized there was a good chance we would enter the fighting in one way or another. We had already provided the Allies with military equipment, and exchanged fifty overage destroyers with Great Britain in return for some naval bases. The month I was activated Congress passed and the President signed the Lend-Lease Act, which I took to mean that the United States was close to war.

Which was why many reserve officers were called to duty, including me. At first, I was ordered to report to the Brooklyn Navy Yard, to the old World War I destroyer the USS *Reuben James*. When I reported to the *Reuben James*, the officer of the deck told me, "Ensign Cullman, your orders are changed," and I was told to report to Washington, D.C., to the Bureau of Navigation—later called the Bureau of Naval Personnel. Two weeks after the change in my assignment, the *Reuben James* went down with almost all hands in the North Atlantic.

In early 1941 Sue and I located a house in Bethesda, Maryland, and settled in with our two-year-old daughter, Dorothy. Sue found a position as a cryptanalyst at Naval Intelligence OP20G.

My job at the time was to be an assistant, processing enlistment and reenlistment applications for the Navy. President Roosevelt had been assistant secretary of the Navy during World War I and understood how important the Navy would be in this war; he was expending every effort to build ships and enlist the personnel to man them. At the time we had the draft; many of the applications I processed were from Navy veterans who expected that in time of war they would be called up, and preferred to return to the Navy rather than be drafted into the Army. So I was quite busy. I had a great volume of applications to process, and most of the time I took action on them without referring the file to my superiors.

One day I received applications from five brothers from Waterloo, Iowa, the Sullivans, who wanted to serve together. I wrote to them saying that it was the Navy's policy not to put more than two members of the same family on one ship. The Sullivans persisted. This went beyond my level of authority, so I went to the senior officer, a lieutenant commander, and asked, "What should I do?"

He thought it over and then, under pressure from a congressman, said, "Enlist them." So I did. All five brothers wound up on the light cruiser *Juneau,* and all died when that ship was sunk off Guadalcanal in late 1942. As it happened, I was on a ship destined for Guadalcanal at that time. The news of what had happened to those boys was one of the most heartrending things I have ever experienced. In 1944 a motion picture based on their lives was released, *The Sullivans.* I couldn't see it; it would have been too painful. It bothers me even now, more than half a century later.

The mood in the office was often tense. My desk was near the offices of Admiral C. W. Nimitz, chief of the bureau. The practice was for one junior officer to serve on duty in his office in case any emergency developed. It was my turn when on May 24, 1941, the admiral was informed that the British battlecruiser HMS *Hood,* considered at the time the most powerful warship in service, was sunk in the North Atlantic by one salvo from the German battleship *Bismarck.* I was told to inform several top naval officers of what had happened. It was a dark day for the U.S. Navy. It showed how strong the German fleet was.

On December 7, 1941, I was at a Washington Redskins football game when a voice came over on the loudspeaker, "Will the Secretary of the Army please report to his office and the Secretary of the Navy please report to his office." Everyone in the stands must have realized something important had happened. After the game the newspaper headlines told the story: "Japanese Bomb Pearl Harbor." I went home, got out my uniform, and reported to my office.

The atmosphere at the Navy Department was one of extreme apprehension. It wasn't until more than three months later that President Roosevelt disclosed the magnitude of the damage done by the Japanese at Pearl Harbor, but we knew right away it was very serious. More than sixty ships, ranging from cruisers and destroyers to battleships, were in the harbor at the time. Fortunately, the fleet's three carriers were at sea, and the Japanese failed to destroy some of the Pearl Harbor fuel tanks and naval repair shops. But around 170 of our planes were destroyed; all our battleships were either sunk or badly damaged; and there were 3,400 casualties. A congressional committee investigating the attack called it "the greatest military and naval disaster in our nation's history." But the public wasn't told about this. Had the Japanese known what some of our top admirals learned within hours of the attack, they might have followed up with an invasion. The extent of the damage inflicted by the Japanese planes remained one of the best-kept secrets of the war until disclosed by FDR.

My designation was "Ensign DVG," which stood for desk volunteer general. In Navy talk that meant I was qualified for sea duty. When I was given the opportunity to do so, I put in for sea duty, and had my choice of large or small ships. I asked for large ships and in the summer of 1942 I was ordered to the USS *Montpelier*, a six-inch-gun cruiser, which was being completed by the New York Ship Building Company in Camden, New Jersey. In order to qualify, I was dispatched to Dam Neck, Virginia, to machine-gun school, and after three days there I became reasonably knowledgeable about 20mm and 40mm machine guns. In the rushed atmosphere of the time, this qualified me as an expert, so when I reported to the *Montpelier* I was immediately designated the machine-gun officer.

The captain was Leighton Wood, a brilliant, experienced, thirty-five year regular Navy man. The sailors loved him and so did I. On December 30, when we crossed the equator en route to Nouméa, New Caledonia, in the South Pacific, the men held the usual ceremonies, one feature of which was that Captain Wood had to "walk the plank," which he did with good humor.

Captain Wood should be given great credit for taking a new ship with an inexperienced crew and forging it into a most successful fighting ship with fifteen battle stars. The *Montpelier* was one of the most active ships in the Navy in World War II with damage from Japanese naval guns, torpedoes, shore batteries, bombs, and kamikazes.

Captain Wood died of natural causes on June 9, 1943, and was buried in the New Hebrides in the South Pacific. He was succeeded by Robert Tobin, a heavyset, gruff man who formerly had commanded destroyers (and had had two sunk under him). Captain Tobin walked with a limp, the result of a battle wound. He was also a fine leader.

Captain Tobin was rotated to the mainland on December 2, 1943, and we got our third skipper, Harry Hoffman, whom we called Harry the Horse behind his back, which wasn't really fair. Hoffman was a conscientious, demanding captain; for this reason, he was not particularly popular, and that's a kind way of putting it. I'm not trying to suggest the situation under Hoffman was anything like some fictional accounts of the war, such as Herman Wouk's *The Caine Mutiny*. We were all quite well behaved. We had the tasks of staying alive, keeping the ship afloat, and contributing to an Allied victory in the war.

As I've mentioned, I was an ensign when the war began. I was promoted to lieutenant junior grade and then lieutenant senior grade after serving the requisite number of months. Neither of these promotions had anything to do with merit. Then I got to be a lieutenant commander, and that was after a commendation from Admiral Aaron "Tip" Merrill. I was promoted to commander in early 1945 by selection, and then I became one of the first Naval Reserve officers to be assigned as a gunnery officer of a new cruiser.

To give you an idea of what a cruiser was like in 1942, the *Montpelier* had a complement of 1,200 men, most of whom were Southerners. The largest department was the gunnery department, with a machine-gun officer, an air defense officer, and a gunnery officer, under whom many other officers served. My battle station, air defense forward, was just above the bridge, so I could often hear and see the captain and Admiral Merrill, Commander Task Force 39, except during action, when we hadn't time to watch.*

The captain of a U.S. warship had all the duties and obligations of the CEO of a mid-sized corporation, and many more, since working in the civilian sector did not involve life-and-death situations. The Navy was quite a change from the cigar business, but then again, it was a unique experience for practically all the men on the ship.

---

*One of the seamen on the *Montpelier* was James J. Fahey, whom I knew. Seaman Fahey kept a diary of his experiences, which was published after the war in several editions. The title is *Pacific War Diary, 1942–1945*. It is one of the outstanding books written about World War II, indispensable for anyone who wants to know what it was like to serve on a warship during the Pacific campaigns. Seaman Fahey will be remembered long after all the rest of us on the *Montpelier* are forgotten.

After more than half a century, many of my memories of the period have faded; others are distorted by time. Because of this, I have relied upon *Pacific War Diary* to stimulate my thoughts on the subject.

We started on our shakedown cruise in Chesapeake Bay, east of Philadelphia. Then, in December 1942, we set sail from Norfolk, Virginia, as part of a convoy of ships bound for the South Pacific via the Panama Canal. The weather in the Atlantic was quite cold and the seas were churning. For quite a few of the men this was their first experience at sea, and seasickness was common. Everything that moved had to be lashed down. We had to eat our meals standing up, because setting tables was impossible. We had a near escape when one of the troopships in the convoy lost a rudder and almost collided with us. But finally we reached warmer climates, and by the time we entered the Caribbean all that was behind us.

The *Montpelier* reached the Panama Canal on December 24, 1942. It took us eight hours to get through the locks to the Pacific. Before departing we anchored off Panama for a brief time. One of my extra duties was motion picture officer, so I went ashore to try to get some films because we wanted to entertain the crew en route to the South Pacific. I managed to get a film starring Rita Hayworth, and we ran it thirty consecutive nights, to a packed audience. I've felt a certain closeness to Rita Hayworth ever since.

The news from the South Pacific was that the Japanese were advancing on all fronts, and the Americans were having a rough time of it. But we were coming back. The Battle of the Coral Sea had taken place in May 1942. This, the first battle in which opposing surface ships were not engaged with each other—all of the fighting was done by planes attacking ships—was not a clear-cut American victory, but it did frustrate the Japanese attempt to seize Port Moresby in southeastern New Guinea and use it as a springboard to invade Australia.

Now we were attempting to turn the tide of battle. The general plan was to stop the Japanese at Guadalcanal in the

Lieutenant Joseph F. Cullman 3rd during World War II.

The USS *Montpelier* after a battle.
Note the spent shell casings on deck.

*Montpelier* personnel watching for a
kamikaze attack.

The officers of the USS *Montpelier* on
the flying bridge. I am fifth from left.

Shore leave, Solomon Islands style.

The cruiser USS *Montpelier* as she looked during World War II.

Admiral "Tip" Merrill, commander of Task Force 39, presents a commendation to me on January 25, 1944.

The officers and men of the USS *Montpelier* assembled topside at Purvis Bay, Solomons, 1944. Note the SOC planes in the background.

Naval officers Joe and Lewis Cullman.

My daughter Dorothy joins me for shore leave in 1944.

O. Parker McComas; my dad, Joseph F. Cullman Jr.; Al Lyon; and I at the signing of the purchase agreement between Philip Morris and Benson & Hedges.

An early Philip Morris meeting. *Left to right:* Hugh Cullman, Bob Roper, O. Parker McComas, myself, George Weissman, and Ross Millhiser.

PM affiliate La Suerte welcomes Sue and me to Manila.

Chairman of FTR Fritz Church, Mario Giorgi of PM, and Frederick Beck of FTR gather with me after the purchase of FTR in Neuchâtel, Switzerland.

The Philip Morris International team. *Left to right:* Aleardo Buzzi, Mario Giorgi, Justus Heymans, and Hugh Cullman.

Chandler Kibbee *(left)* stands with me and the PM team in Switzerland in the late 1960s.

Nearly a half century of Philip Morris leadership. *Left to right:* Cliff Goldsmith, John Murphy, myself, Tom Ahrensfeld, Shep Pollack, George Weissman, and in front, the famous Johnny Roventini.

*Left to right:* Former PM chairmen George Weissman and Bill Murray; PM chairman Geoff Bible; and former PM chairmen Joseph F. Cullman 3rd and Hamish Maxwell.

Solomon Islands, then work our way "up the ladder," first taking the Solomons, which cover more than 500 miles, then the Gilberts, the Marianas, and the Bonin Islands, which would take us within bombing range of the Japanese home islands. The strategy worked well; we captured Iwo Jima and Okinawa in 1945, as the last part of the plan. That was the big picture.

Anti-aircraft gunnery practice became an important part of my life. Our planes would tow targets and I would direct our anti-aircraft gunners to fire at them. We hoped to be ready for action when the time came.

Life aboard a warship in the South Pacific alternated between periods of intense action and intense boredom. When we were in combat, we craved boredom, and when we were bored, we looked forward to action. When we were not in action, a typical day began with reveille, which was at 4:50 A.M., followed by gunnery drill. Breakfast was at 6:20, followed by more drills and inspections. Lunch began at 11:15 A.M., in shifts, followed by inspections and more drills. We had supper beginning at 5:00 P.M., and then if we were at sea all hands manned their general quarters battle stations one hour before sunset. After dark, we might watch a movie when the enemy was not near. There were books and magazines; I read a lot of Hemingway, Galsworthy, and Dickens novels. We again manned general quarters one hour before sunrise.

The South Pacific was tough duty, not only because of the fighting but because of the weather. The heat could be a killer, but worse than that was the rain. This region has some of the heaviest rainfall in the world. I used to stand up on my battle station and it would rain so hard that the water would come above my knees, despite the drains.

We arrived in Nouméa, New Caledonia, a French possession in the hands of the Free French, on January 18, 1943.

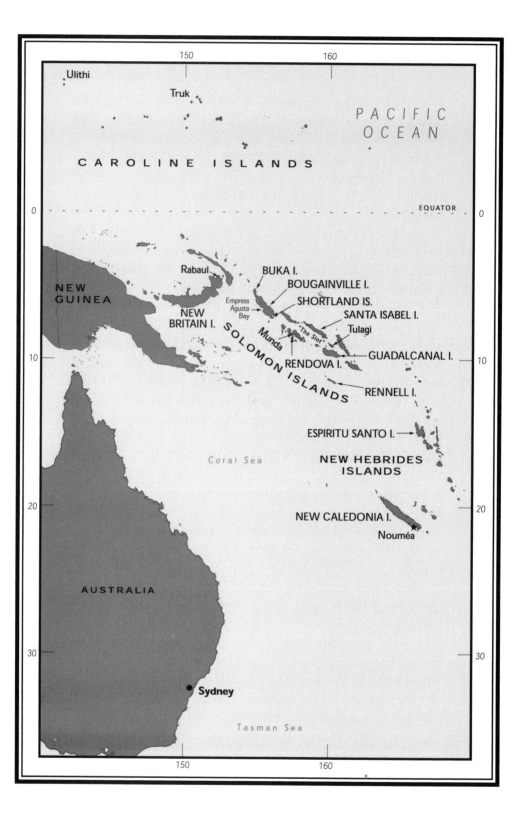

En route we had checked out the batteries and performed all sorts of drills to prepare for the unknown. Nouméa is about 900 nautical miles northeast of Australia; the *Montpelier* arrived there after more than month at sea. The men had shore leave, and were able to purchase fruit from the locals, which was a welcome change for us. To say it was unusual was to understate the impact the place had on us, for most of the men had never ventured that far from home. Now they came into contact with a small Melanesian people whose culture and customs they didn't understand. They looked into the lagoons and watched the tail fins of sharks. When able to swim, they did so in the company of tropical fish some of them might have seen in pet shops. It was all quite exotic.

The *Montpelier* had not been present for the first stage of the grand strategy, which began in January 1942, but the campaign was to be a long one. The action really got going when the Marines landed on Guadalcanal in August 1942, one of the most southerly of the Solomons, east of New Guinea, and then later on Bougainville, northwest of Guadalcanal. The *Montpelier* had joined an American force and some British vessels in Nouméa, so we knew something important was going to take place. I was able to go ashore one night; the next day, though, our flotilla, consisting of four cruisers and eight destroyers, steamed out of the harbor heading north toward Guadalcanal, where we planned to rendezvous with the rest of the task force, commanded by Admiral Merrill. It was January 27, 1943. That night we experienced our first action, an attack by twenty-two Japanese twin-engine "Betty" bombers.

We got into more action on January 31, south of Guadalcanal near Rennell Island. The Japanese sent in air reinforcements from Rabaul, on the island of New Britain, and hit one of our heavy cruisers, the *Chicago,* with two torpedoes. To assist the *Chicago,* we threw out a line and started towing her. With this the Japanese attacked both ships, their planes strafing us with machine-gun fire. Their planes came in waves. The *Chicago* went down after being hit by two more torpedoes, and Japanese planes also badly damaged the destroyer *La Vallette*. We were constantly in action, trying to remain alert and get the job done, constantly having to make split-second decisions. None of us got much sleep for two days, and we ate when possible.

The *Montpelier* next joined in the action around Guadalcanal, where the land fighting lasted until February 1943, by which time the American forces had secured the island. In mid February we were still assigned to Merrill's Task Force 39, comprising three light cruisers and eight destroyers, part of the Third Fleet commanded by Admiral William "Bull" Halsey. Our task was to participate in the battle for Munda, a small island just off New Georgia, which lies north and west of Guadalcanal. We fired six-inch and five-inch guns at the Japanese ships and fortifications.

No one who hasn't been in such a situation can really understand what it fells like when your ship seems to be surrounded by exploding shells. These actions around Munda went on until early March, when we were ordered back to Espiritu Santo for repairs. Although our marksmanship had improved, there were more exercises, shooting at towline targets. And sometimes we served as practice targets. Planes from the carrier USS *Saratoga* made mock attacks on the *Montpelier*.

After two weeks in Espiritu Santo we were back at sea, to intercept Japanese ships that might attack our base on Guadalcanal, which the Japanese were trying to retake. In late June 1943, Task Force 39 joined a large task force and went to a part of the Solomons known as the Slot, a narrow band of the sea between Santa Isabel Island and New Georgia. We called it the Slot because there were Japanese forces on both sides of the channel and there was very little room to maneuver. The Japanese knew what was happening, and each night were on guard against us. This time the task force went up the Slot to bombard the Shortland Islands to the northwest as part of a diversion, while the main force was to land on the island of Rendova to the south. All this to capture the critical Solomon Islands, one at a time. It was a dangerous task. The *Montpelier* was hit by a torpedo—fortunately, a dud. And then back to Espiritu Santo to take on supplies, before returning to sea to assist in the final taking of Rendova.

By then I suppose we had become accustomed to this kind of life. Rarely did anyone get a full night's sleep. We never knew when we would be able to eat, so our pockets usually contained candy bars. I often ate a raw-onion sandwich for lunch. We were often hungry, since you can't stop to eat in battle. The heat was oppressive. Imagine what it's like on an all-metal ship that has no air conditioning and has been baking in the tropical sun for months. Add tropical humidity and 1,200 men. It was *very* hot. The rainstorms were short but powerful. Then, weary, sweating, and hungry, we would find ourselves back in action, and the adrenaline would flow as the Japanese planes and ships attacked.

While at Espiritu Santo, southeast of Guadalcanal, we learned that the cruiser task force that relieved us had been attacked. Three of our light cruisers had been damaged, one badly (the *Helena*). The destroyer *Gwin* was sunk, and some other destroyers had been put out of action. At times like that, Yale and the cigar business seemed part of a very different existence. All that went before seemed at the same time both precious and irrelevant. I have spoken to others who have had combat experience, and they had similar feelings.

Friday, September 3, 1943, was an important date for the crew of the *Montpelier*. For the first time in ten months we spent a whole day on shore, at Espiritu Santo. All the other times we had dropped anchor there, we would make repairs, take on ammunition and other supplies, and then go back to sea. Some of the men hadn't stepped off the ship in more than half a year. Most of them headed to food stands to buy hot dogs and soft drinks; others went swimming in the lagoon or went for strolls in the jungle, where they picked and ate fresh fruit. We played softball, basketball, and other games. We even saw our first women that year.

Eleanor Roosevelt was on a tour of the Pacific front at that time. She spoke to us for about ten minutes and then went through our ship, stopping to talk to sailors in a friendly and natural way. As she did so, troop ships were being loaded and C-46 and C-47 transport planes were being prepared for the assault on Bougainville, the most northerly island in the Solomon archipelago, manned by some 40,000 Japanese soldiers.

We steamed out of Espiritu Santo late in September 1943 to join in the preliminaries of the attack on Bougainville. On the way we saw a large fire on one of the islands. The Japanese would light those fires, hoping an American ship would fire on them and give away its position. Waiting submerged would be one of their submarines which, on seeing the gunfire, would know the location of the American ship and fire torpedoes at it. Captain Tobin knew about this trick and didn't fall for it. We were back in Espiritu Santo by early October, and then joined a large task force with five battleships, a reassuring sight.

On October 15 we heard the news that we would be going to Australia for liberty; four days later we pulled into Sydney Harbor along with a destroyer escort. October is springtime in Australia, and the weather was just right—a respite from the humid, rainy world we had been in for so long. The next time I would go to Australia would be as a PM executive, but this first visit was something special. Espiritu Santo was fine in its way, but it wasn't Western civilization.

Now we could walk on paved streets, see tall buildings, and shop in real stores. Sydney had a population then of around 2 million. It resembled many American cities, and of course the people there spoke English. The Australians were very much like Americans, only friendlier, warmer, and more open. Needless to say, given the circumstances, the *Montpelier* contingent was delighted with the local girls more than anything else.

One of the things that I noticed immediately was how much the Australians liked American cigarettes. The sailors would smuggle them off the ship as presents for their Australian friends.

We left Sydney on October 25. Four days later we arrived at Tulagi in the Solomons, and two days after that were back at sea. Our task force bombarded Japanese installations at Buka and Buin in the northwest part of Bougainville, and then sailed south to bombard the Shortlands. All these actions were diversions, aimed at making the Japanese think we were mounting a major effort there, when in fact the main force was heading toward Bougainville, and we would head there too.

In the history books it is sometimes called the Battle of Empress Augusta Bay, which was the major port on the southwest side of the island. The *Montpelier* was the flagship in this November 2, 1943 night action, which included some of the toughest fighting we had seen so far. Salvos were landing all around us. The Japanese were firing torpedoes at our ships, and our destroyers were doing the same at their ships. We could see torpedo wakes in the water, for though it was night, all of that firing, plus the star shells being fired by both sides, made it bright. We could sometimes see the fins of giant sharks, circling around.

On the morning of November 2, our task force was attacked by about seventy Japanese planes, mostly Val dive-bombers, and we opened up with our five-inch, 40mm and 20mm anti-aircraft guns. They did some damage to us, but we prevailed. When some Japanese pilots bailed out, some of our men shot them. Afterward we were berated for this violation of the Articles of War. In their defense, our sailors said they knew the Japanese had done this to our pilots, and were retaliating. It sounds barbaric today, but it didn't seem that way in 1943.

The Battle of Empress Augusta Bay resulted in a decisive American victory; soon after, Rabaul on New Britain to the northwest, the major Japanese base in the South Pacific, was isolated, its airfield and harbor useless. This meant the Japanese would have to retire to their large naval base at Truk Island 700 nautical miles north. The Solomons were not completely secured until early 1944, as the Japanese troops retreated to the lush, almost impenetrable jungle. Some continued to fight on even after the war ended.

The *Montpelier* was now assigned to Admiral Marc Mitscher's Task Force 58, in the Fifth Fleet under Admiral Raymond Spruance. When we learned of this, we also knew where we were going. For weeks there had been talk that the Fifth was going to lead the way to the Marianas—Guam, Tinian, Saipan—up the ladder to the Japanese home islands. Because the Marianas were an obvious target, some said Admiral Spruance would go after Truk, while others said the first battlefield would be Guam. Scuttlebutt had it that General MacArthur had convinced President Roosevelt that we should retake the Philippines instead. MacArthur had said, "I shall return," when he left the Philippines, and he fairly ached to make his word good.

While we were still wondering which it was to be, the *Montpelier* participated in an exercise to put out of operation some Japanese pillboxes with large guns that remained on Bougainville. We finally said good-bye to the Solomons in

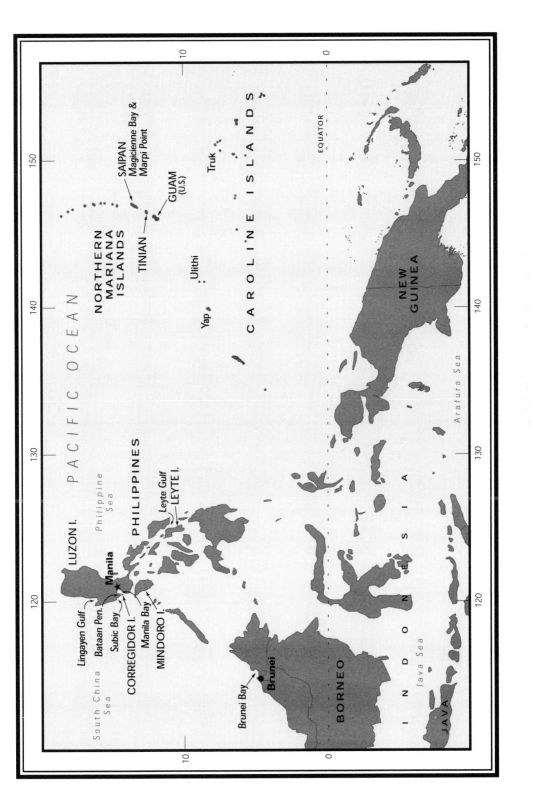

May 1944. We'd been there for eighteen months, except for the liberty in Sydney. The *Montpelier* was a lucky ship, coming through the campaign relatively unscathed. The Solomons were now secure.

We set off to join the Fifth Fleet. While en route to Saipan we learned of the June 6, 1944, landing in Normandy, and during the next few days we heard it was a success. Maybe the war in Europe was winding down, I thought, and if so, we would get more supplies and manpower, and bring the Pacific War to a faster conclusion.

Saipan, our target in the Marianas, was a major Japanese stronghold. Taking Saipan might be tougher than Guadalcanal or Bougainville. The only comfort we had was that as we sailed north the weather improved. It was June, and we used blankets at night. Quite a change from the Solomons.

Shortly after June 6, 1944, D-Day, we started bombarding Saipan, softening it up for the invasion. The *Montpelier* fired its five-inch and six-inch guns almost steadily for three days, and the continual concussions eventually shook parts of our communications bridge loose. The task force fired at everything on the island—storage tanks, ammunition dumps, railroads, outbuildings. One of the *Montpelier*'s five-inch guns took out a Japanese twin five-inch turret at Magicienne Bay by placing a shell through their gun turret opening. Meanwhile our planes were bombing and strafing the island, and spotting targets for the ships.

The Japanese threw the works at us. The *Montpelier* was attacked by kamikazes, shore batteries, naval gunfire. At one point we were straddled. We had enemy shells landing on both sides of the ship. I saw splashes fifty yards away on one side and fifty yards on the other. This was serious. But we were giving better than we were taking. The Marines had landed, but ran into heavy gunfire that caused many casualties. We didn't hang around for long, however.

A few days later the *Montpelier* joined a force sent to intercept a large Japanese naval flotilla dispatched to engage us and thwart the invasion. On the way, we learned that Tokyo was being bombed by B-29s based in China. Soon we were joined by other ships, a task force that stretched as far as I could see. Later I learned that practically the entire Fifth Fleet was there.

We engaged the Japanese force on June 19 west of Saipan with the *Montpelier* in the unenviable position of lead ship. Japanese planes filled the sky, coming from all directions. We took some damage and human losses, but our planes also did heavy damage. Some 600 Japanese planes were downed, mostly by our airpower, and many of their ships were badly damaged, including four carriers, one of which was sunk. All this only 600 or so miles from the Japanese home islands. The Japanese flotilla withdrew, as planes from our carriers pursued them.

By June 20, low on fuel and ammunition, we awaited supplies of both. It was a beautiful day, and the men lolled on the deck, resting from the battles. It seemed bizarre. As I mentioned earlier, interludes of strenuous fighting were broken by periods of silence and calm.

After the provisioning was completed, the *Montpelier* was back in action bombarding Saipan. I saw hundreds of Japanese soldiers, about to be overrun, jumping off a cliff at Marpi Point on the north tip of Saipan, into the sea. Then followed the invasions of Tinian on July 18 and Guam on July 21. They were not as difficult. And Saipan had been completely in our hands since July 10.

Around this time rumors spread through the ship that we were heading back to the United States. On August 2, Captain Hoffman told us that we were going to the Marshalls for a few days, then on to Pearl Harbor; from there, we'd head to San Francisco for repairs and shore leaves.

The return to the U.S. was very exciting. Steaming under

the Golden Gate Bridge in San Francisco was a thrill. The *Monty* went to Mare Island for repairs, and I went back to Washington to be met at the airport after eighteen months away by Sue and our daughter, Dorothy—a great family experience.

We then went to Kildare near Tupper Lake in the Adirondacks for a great week. After all that sea and jungle, I wanted to see coniferous and deciduous trees. I had always enjoyed the outdoors, and this was an important emotional experience. I rested, slept, walked, fished, and, most important, got to know my family again. I knew my leave would be short, but by then it appeared the war was winding down into its final phase. Still, there was no way of predicting what would happen. Ahead in Europe was the German counterattack that led to the Battle of the Bulge, and in the Pacific many people expected that the invasion of the Japanese home islands might cost us more than a million casualties. Back in San Francisco, I helped supervise the refitting of the ship. We were at Mare Island from August 22 through October 25, 1944—long enough to feel the war was over. Nevertheless, we had to return to the Pacific. The *Montpelier* was completely repaired and re-outfitted with new guns.

By October 1944, it seemed—falsely, as it turned out—that the war in Europe was close to its end. American forces had entered Germany. The Pacific War was going very well indeed. General MacArthur was headed back to the Philippines, and on Saipan the Seabees were completing work on the airstrips from which the B-29s would take off to bomb the Japanese home islands. At the time of our departure from Pearl Harbor, there was the major battle of Leyte Gulf, in the Philippines, in which the Japanese navy was crushed, losing three battleships, four carriers, six cruisers, and fourteen destroyers. We didn't know it then, but this was the last important surface naval battle of the war, for the simple reason that the Japanese had been so badly hurt by their losses in the Philippine naval campaign.

In October 1944, the *Montpelier* sailed from San Francisco on the same kind of cold, blustery day it had been when we made our first trip in 1942. En route we spent much time in gunnery practice, needed because we were rusty from the layoff. When we arrived in Pearl Harbor there was more practice and breaking in new equipment. Then we set out for the Philippines, to assist in the taking of additional islands in that archipelago.

We pulled into Ulithi, a Western Pacific atoll a hundred-odd miles northeast of Yap; there we learned that our destination was Leyte in the Philippines, the scene of our major victory in October. We joined the Seventh Fleet, under the command of Bull Halsey. Captain Hoffman told us there were plenty of Japanese PT boats in the area, as well as submarines and planes, but not many surface ships. Their planes caused us trouble; many kamikazes attacked us and we were hit by three of them, but survived the attacks.

In December the *Montpelier* participated in the invasion of Mindoro, a Philippine island south of Manila's island, Luzon. Apparently what remained of the Japanese fleet in that part of the Pacific was lurking in the area, and our job was to prevent them from harassing our carriers. As it happened, our troops caught the Japanese land force on Mindoro by surprise, and the landing took place without opposition. Our task force downed many Japanese planes and more were destroyed on the ground by our planes. We didn't see any Japanese ships, and we suspected there weren't many of them in the area.

With Mindoro secured, we headed back to Leyte for supplies and munitions, and to prepare for the taking of Luzon. This would enable MacArthur to make his triumphal return as promised. He was on the light cruiser *Boise*; en route to Lingayen Gulf north of Manila all of us kept our eyes on that ship when we weren't busy fighting off Japanese planes.

We spent Christmas 1944 at sea, and celebrated with a

fine meal. We all knew that barring anything unusual, we would be home next Christmas.

There were close to 850 transports and supply ships in the Lingayen Gulf invasion, along with many warships and small craft. It was to be one of the biggest invasions of the Pacific War. The first U.S. attack wave met with light opposition. Japanese planes were there attempting to strafe and bomb. Encounters with the Japanese were getting lighter all the time, except for the kamikazes, a sure indication that the war was drawing to a close.

The *Montpelier* was then involved in the action that led to MacArthur's "return" to the Philippines, which he had promised three years earlier. First, our forces retook Subic Bay, north of Bataan. The next step was the attack on Corregidor itself by ships and paratroopers. Corregidor guards the approaches to Manila Bay. It was there that Admiral Dewey defeated the Spanish in 1898 and gave the famous command "You may fire when ready, Gridley."

The retaking of Corregidor was an important strategic and psychological move. MacArthur had been surrounded by Japanese forces in early 1942 and had just escaped from Corregidor to Australia by PT boat. Many American troops were captured, and many of those died on the infamous Bataan death march.

This time, after heavy close-in fighting, our troops finally retook Corregidor from the Japanese. The *Montpelier* was offshore, providing support as the action swept across the island. At one point, as I looked over the side, I saw a Japanese soldier swimming toward our ship with a grenade in one hand, showing every intention of getting close enough to throw the grenade toward Admiral Merrill on the bridge. The Marines on the *Montpelier* dispatched the soldier.

For most of February we participated in mopping-up operations and repairs. We saw some strange and tragic sights.

We liberated hundreds of American prisoners from Japanese prison camps. They resembled the pictures of Jewish inmates of German death camps. The Filipinos told us stories about Japanese atrocities. A great deal of attention was given, rightly so, to the German atrocities. But even if the Japanese atrocities were on a smaller scale, they were just as brutal and inhuman.

We also heard of American soldiers who took to the hills and jungles after the Japanese invasion of Luzon in 1941, and had been fighting there, alongside Filipinos, for the past three years. When permitted to do so, we visited Manila, which was supposed to have been one of the world's most beautiful cities. It was no longer so; the Japanese had ripped apart everything they could and burned the rest before leaving.

None of us who went through these experiences on Luzon felt any remorse when we heard of the dropping of the atomic bombs on Hiroshima and Nagasaki to shorten the war and prevent a million or more Allied casualties.

The *Montpelier* remained in the Philippines until June, when it left to participate in the landings at Brunei Bay in Borneo. After that, for me the fighting war was over. I received orders to the effect that "Commander Joseph Cullman is detached from the USS *Montpelier* and is to proceed by available means and report to the New York Shipbuilding Company in Camden, New Jersey, to become the gunnery officer of the USS *Charleston*." I returned by ship to Pearl Harbor and then by airplane to the U.S.A.

The war ended on August 14, 1945, before I could report to the *Charleston*. Since I had been in the Navy for four and a half years, I was eligible for early release. I put in my papers and went on inactive duty in November. By then I was looking forward eagerly to my return to the tobacco business, but also wanted to explore some other ideas that occurred to me during the war.

After 1945 I reflected that my generation had gone

through some very tough and agonizing experiences in the war, and many of my friends lost their lives or their health, but for those of us who lived through it, it was one of the most valuable educational experiences in our lives. This certainly is not a brief for war itself, which is a horrible experience. But I feel that I learned as much about life, the world, and myself in the months in the South Pacific as I did in all my years in school and college.

I once read that there are 8 million veterans of World War II still alive, and that more than 11 million Americans were on active duty when the war ended. Many of us have tough memories of the war, but over time some of those have faded; and, for me at least, the war provided an important experience. Some of the good memories derive from the passage of time, but also we always knew what we were fighting for from 1941 to 1945. There was very little jingoism in World War II, but rather a grim determination to get it over with and to destroy what all of us considered a truly evil enemy. We knew we were fighting to save democracy.

I can sympathize with Korean War veterans who say they fought to a draw and lives were lost in an uncertain cause, and even more with Vietnam veterans, whose stories are too familiar to bear retelling. As I have already indicated, I still keep in touch with some of the men I met during the war, especially those who served on the *Montpelier*. I attend reunions when possible; we correspond, and meet whenever we can. It was an important part of our lives.

# CHAPTER THREE

# Marlboro Country: The Beginning

*Business has only two basic functions—*
*marketing and innovation.*

—Peter Drucker

IN 1945 MILLIONS OF VETERANS faced the problems of readjusting to civilian life. Like so many of them, I wasn't as sure of my future now as I had been at the time I entered the Navy. Everything seemed so simple in 1940. I would continue on at Webster, and in time, assuming I could cut the mustard, might succeed Dad as head of the firm. It was in the Cullman tradition, but I had been doing a lot of thinking while aboard the *Montpelier* from 1942 to 1945. I often wondered how we in America got to where we were as a people and what I should do with my life.

Before World War II, I had found the tobacco business very interesting and rewarding. Now, after that tour in the Pacific, tobacco didn't seem as important as it once had. I always had loved history, and I considered returning to a university, obtaining a Ph.D., and seeking a career teaching at a college or school. So when we returned to New York in 1945 and settled down, I enrolled in an American history colloquium at Columbia University, before deciding to work with Dad at Benson & Hedges.

On my return I discovered that little Benson & Hedges had prospered during the war. This wasn't unusual; all the cigarette firms had done well, since people smoked more during war. Military sales alone were staggering. In 1945, when there were 12 million men and women in the service, military sales accounted for 65 billion units, or 10 percent of U.S. output. In this kind of atmosphere, and given the wartime prosperity, civilians didn't mind spending a little more for the premium brands turned out by B&H.

Dad was now in his mid-sixties and still going strong, but he had no desire to expand the company to the point where it might pose a challenge to the industry's large firms. Old Gold and even Philip Morris might compete against Lucky Strike and Camel, but Parliament was in an entirely different league. Dad quite frankly used snob appeal. "Be Lady Astor for an extra dime," he would say, and it worked.

Parliament's classy cardboard boxes, the filter mouthpiece, and the cotton filter were hard to make during the war, and B&H had to ration them to dealers. Dad gave more attention to Virginia Rounds, which were offered in the conventional cup package. In 1945 B&H reported sales of $5.3 million, a record that was soon to be shattered. Now that the war was over Parliament was able to expand to meet demand.

This was the situation I found on returning from the Navy in the fall of 1945. I recall going to the small Benson & Hedges factory on Water Street. The machines were slow, in part because the B&H brands were more difficult to manufacture than ordinary cigarettes, but also because the machines were by then old and subject to even more frequent breakdowns than had been the case before the war. There was no air-conditioning in the factory, and during summer months the heat was fierce, affecting not only the workers, but the machines themselves. The workers were mostly first-generation immigrants, Hispanic men and women. There was still a labor shortage at that time.

Early on I met Cliff Goldsmith, a man who would have a profound effect upon me. Cliff took a convoluted path to Benson & Hedges. On the eve of World War II he was in England, where he received a degree in textile engineering. He was in Stockholm when the war broke out in Europe. The Goldsmith family, German Jews, went from there to Moscow, then via the Trans-Siberian Railroad to Vladivostok, and then on to Tokyo and the United States. He worked for a while at a textile plant in New York, entered the Army when America got into the war in 1941, joined an intelligence unit, and wound up in Italy, where he was captured and sent to a prison camp. When the war ended Cliff was freed; he returned to the United States to be discharged.

Before entering the Army Cliff had met my brother Arthur, who was working for Philip Morris. Arthur was very much taken with Cliff. By the time the war was over Arthur had gone to Benson & Hedges; he asked Cliff to leave the textile business and come to work for B&H. Cliff must have thought there was more of a future in tobacco than in textiles, so he accepted the offer.

One of Cliff's tasks was to speed up the slow old Himoff machines, or makers, as they were called, so B&H could meet the growing demand for its cigarettes. When he arrived, the machines were turning out 125 cigarettes a minute. In order to understand what this means, consider that today's machines produce more than 10,000 a minute. Cliff made constant improvements, and was highly regarded in the company by the time I got there. He was a fine engineer.

Dad and Cliff clashed over the purchase of additional machinery. Cliff always wanted more; Dad always fought back. "You're not going to get another cent out of me," Dad would roar. Cliff would roar back, and more often than not, he succeeded, because Dad knew he was right. We needed those machines if we were to grow the business.

Cliff was also mastering the intricacies of tobacco blending and manufacturing. He was a fast learner. At the time of his retirement, he was one of the top executives at Philip Morris and an expert on leaf, manufacturing, and machinery. Such was the quality of people I found on arriving at B&H in 1945. I soon became intrigued by the business, and gradually the plan to become a teacher seemed less attractive than it had when I left the Navy.

As interest in filters grew, demand for Parliaments continued to expand, even after the wartime shortages ended. Parliament was not widely advertised in this period; the brand was generally available only in better outlets.

We soon learned the reason for Parliament's new popularity: some New York doctors had been recommending them to their patients for health reasons. Those who opposed smoking cigarettes said they might cause sore throats or cut down on your wind or your life expectancy. Athletes were warned against smoking in those days; that was the extent of the health issue. But scientific papers were appearing exploring the possible links between smoking and a variety of ailments. Some doctors were urging their patients to stop smoking, or failing that, to smoke a filter brand, which they assumed delivered less tar and nicotine. Parliament, with its cotton filter, which as I mentioned was placed there more to keep bits of tobacco from sticking to the smoker's lips than to screen tar and nicotine, thus became more popular, along with Viceroy.

Had we been American Tobacco or R. J. Reynolds, this added business would have been reason to pump up production. But not at Benson & Hedges. Dad had to engage in serious soul-searching in 1946. He had always wanted to be small, to know every nook and cranny of his business. Now he was faced with a chance to become bigger than he had ever been either in cigarettes or cigars. Toward the end of his career he had to make product and business choices that would have troubled a much younger man. Understandably, he moved slowly and cautiously, but he did move.

For one thing, he decided to put me in charge of the sales effort. That sounded fine; I was now thirty-four years old, and eager to catch up on those years away from business. But I knew Dad was a tough boss. He was very demanding, as he had been to my brothers. Working for your father is never easy, I suppose. Years later I was told a story about Calvin Coolidge, Jr., who was laboring under the hot sun in the Hatfield, Massachusetts, tobacco fields. He mentioned to his co-workers that he was the President's son. "Gee, if the President was my father, I wouldn't be working here," said one of the laborers. "You would, if your father were my father," was the reply. Calvin Coolidge and my father had that in common.

We started advertising—not much, but enough to bring the Parliament name to people around New York who had never heard of it. Our small ads were placed in prestigious magazines like *Cue* and *The New Yorker*. This level of advertising was modest enough, but it was quite costly for a small company like B&H. By 1949 our advertising budget came to $300,000, which was 50 cents for every 1,000 cigarettes we sold. To clarify what this figure means: the big guns of the industry spent much more, but they also sold a lot more cigarettes than we did, so they averaged 20 cents per 1,000.

Our ads were in good taste, designed to appeal to the upscale customers we hoped to reach. There was no shouting and yelling, none of the testimonials that were so common in that period, no hype. Instead, we were content to have our ads say things like "removes much of the tar—keeps all loose bits of tobacco from reaching your lips." There were no doctors' endorsements. Nevertheless, I knew that doctors had made their contribution in a much more important way to Parliament's success. This classy advertising was created by Bob Lusk of Benton & Bowles, one of the industry's top people.

We hired a very small sales force of about a dozen that concentrated its efforts in urban markets. It took only a matter of months before customers in the more exclusive retail outlets in such cities as Los Angeles and Chicago, and in parts of Florida and New England, were able to buy the distinctive Parliament cigarettes.

Sales rose dramatically. In fact, at that point we were both the smallest and the fastest-growing company in the industry. Our sales reached $3.9 million in 1947, $4.9 million in 1948 and, in 1949, $7.2 million. This growth did not mean we were competing with the big companies. Consider that in 1949, American Tobacco had sales of $859 million; R. J. Reynolds, $746 million; Liggett & Myers, $556 million; Philip Morris, $256 million; and Lorillard, $153 million.

In 1949, Camel, the leading American brand, sold 97 billion cigarettes; Lucky Strike was in second place with 93 billion. Even Fatima, a now forgotten exotic cigarette out of Liggett & Myers, which like Parliament sold in a few communities, sold 1.5 billion cigarettes. Taken together, between Parliament and Virginia Rounds, our brands accounted for 600 million cigarettes out of industry sales of 353 billion. This was about one fifth of 1 percent share.

We weren't in the big time, or a threat to the leaders. Even so, they must have envied some of our numbers, and if imitation is the purest form of flattery, we should have been highly complimented. Into the market came Du Maurier, Encore, and Lords, all aimed at our premium-priced market. In 1937 a new company, Riggio Tobacco, had come out with Regent, which was also in a crushproof cardboard box but lacked a filter or cardboard mouthpiece. Regent enjoyed some success, but we'd gotten there first, and with a different and superior cigarette, so Parliament sales continued to climb.

Thanks largely to the success of Parliament, B&H was faced with the need to expand its manufacturing facilities. We purchased a second factory in Yonkers, with Cliff Goldsmith handling most of the work on that project. And in 1953 we were considering yet another one. Sales for 1953 were nearly five times the 1948 figure: more than $27 million, on which B&H earned a profit of $1.2 million. Assets that year were $15.9 million. But for the shareholders there was a price for this growth. We had paid a nominal dividend in 1949 and 1950, but nothing in 1951–53, since we needed cash for expansion. In 1953 we did provide stockholders with the rights to purchase, at $23.50, one new share for every ten they owned. At that time, the market price was in the high 20s, and within a year the stock had doubled. My father couldn't help but be pleased with this.

By then I was directing the efforts of around twenty sales representatives in the major U.S. markets. From next to nothing when I arrived, now we had an effective team. In the process I had learned a good deal about marketing, and by then was considered prepared for bigger things. I had earned a good reputation within the industry, and were it not for the fact that I was in a family business I might have moved on to a position at one of the tobacco industry's major firms.

Dad might have disagreed with my assessment. He liked to say that it was the cigarette, the packaging, the filter mouthpiece, and other such unique qualities that sold Parliament, not so much what I had done with marketing the brand. This didn't bother me. He was a devoted, loving father to all his children, but when it came to the business, he could be a tiger. We had learned to expect this, and accepted the attitude as just another part of his personality.

It was around this time that a new development—or, to be more precise, a new form of an old problem—hit the cigarette industry. It was to alter things at Benson & Hedges and change my life markedly. It was the smoking and health issue.

I would like to indicate how it affected B&H in 1954. To do so, I will have to talk about the climate on this issue in the early 1950s.

The health issue has been around almost as long as the introduction of tobacco to Europe by Columbus. The most famous early attack on tobacco came in 1604, when England's King James I anonymously issued his "A Counter-Blaste to Tobacco," in which he spoke of the "stinking" practice, disputed medicinal claims, and ended his statement by describing smoking as "A custom loathsome to the eye, hateful to the nose, harmful to the brain, dangerous to the lungs, and the black stinking fume thereof, nearest resembling the horrible stygian smoke of the pit that is bottomless."

Lucy Page Gaston, a nineteenth-century reformer, waged a campaign against tobacco, asserting that an agent she called furfural in cigarette tobacco caused smokers to develop "cigarette face," which she claimed could be easily spotted. Those who inhaled a great deal of tobacco smoke would turn to drink, become diseased, take to crime, and in the end, die horribly. Gaston scoured the newspapers for negative items relating to cigarettes; she would then rewrite them and attempt to place the doctored pieces in other newspapers. A typical article, which she said was based on something she read in the *Denver Post*, was this: "Daffy: John Jones, aged 19, is very sick and at times acts very queer: caused by the excessive use of cigarettes."

In time Gaston's crusade petered out, but before it did

she attempted to run for the presidency on an anticigarette platform in 1920, claiming that the Republican nominee, Warren Harding, had cigarette face. She said he would die in office—which, of course, he did.

Cigarette makers realized that while most people considered Gaston a harmless crank, some consumers experienced irritations and others worried about the adverse effects of inhaling. To try to win smokers to their brands, manufacturers attempted to address such concerns. One of the most effective campaigns was run by Lucky Strike in the late 1920s. Well-known actors, actresses, and sports figures were used in advertisements, offering such advice as "Reach for a Lucky instead of a sweet." Lucky Strike ads said "Toasting frees Lucky Strike from impurities. 20,679 physicians recognize this when they say Luckies are less irritating than other cigarettes. Athletes who must keep fit, testify that Luckies do not harm their wind nor physical condition. That's why Luckies have always been the favorite of those men who want to keep in tip-top shape and realize the danger of overweight. That's why folks say: 'It's good to smoke Luckies.'"

Even then there was this problem. Smokers enjoyed cigarettes, but they had nagging suspicions that smoking might be harmful. So the anticigarette movement never completely died out. As I've indicated, one of the reasons Parliament sales rose was because of doctors' recommendations in the 1950s. Increasingly researchers attempted to link smoking with human health problems.

In 1952 a small, largely unknown journal called the *Christian Herald* published some articles dealing with the alleged health consequences of smoking. Most were by Roy Norr, the editor of an anticigarette publication called *Smoking and Health News*. In one of the articles Norr charged that the "medical bureaucracy" was helping the tobacco industry "obscure the truth." In other words, there was a conspiracy. These articles were examples of preaching to the converted. At the time I hadn't heard of either publication, or of Roy Norr.

But DeWitt and Lila Wallace knew of them. The Wallaces were publishers and editors of *Reader's Digest*, the magazine with the largest circulation in the United States. Millions of middle-class Americans looked to the Wallaces' staff to go through the month's newspapers and magazines and present them with what was worth reading. *Reader's Digest* had a reputation for excellent editing and rewriting, but it also had been accused of placing what the Wallaces considered important stories in magazines so as to be able to reprint them later on. Whether this was the case with the Norr articles is unknown, but a synopsis of some of them appeared in the *Reader's Digest* issue of December 1952, under the title "Cancer by the Carton."

This was part of a long crusade the Wallaces had been conducting against cigarettes. In December 1941, for example, *Reader's Digest* had published an article entitled "Nicotine Knockout," supposedly by former boxing champion Gene Tunney, who said that if you smoked, "you will have many diseases and die young." In July of the following year it ran another article, "Cigarette Advertising Fact and Fiction," claiming that cigarettes were essentially all the same, and were deadly.

"Cancer by the Carton" upped the ante. Never before had the *Digest* made so specific and damaging an assertion. And the article contained a demand for action. Antitobacco forces wanted to alarm the public on the basis of their own biased views. This was a blow at the industry.

So began what one writer called the Cigarette Wars. *Reader's Digest* would publish many more articles on this subject, but the December 1952 piece was the one that set things off. In articles the following year such statements as

"ACS Nails Smoking as Cancer Cause" were made. The American Cancer Society had done no such thing. But many casual readers believed there was a link.

One of the reactions was to consider a step up in the promotion of king-sized cigarettes, since the longer product would filter the smoke more than did the regular-sized one. More promising was the idea of a filter built into each cigarette. All the major companies embarked on crash programs to develop filters. We were selling Parliaments as fast as they could be turned out. By 1953 we had more than 600 employees and were bursting at the seams. Dad positively glowed. He had purchased a hobby and found it to be a gold mine.

I felt otherwise. Parliament was doing splendidly, all right, but while those *Reader's Digest* articles were partly responsible for our present successes, they also could destroy us. We were big in a very small market—the market for filtered cigarettes; B&H could never hope to be a major player in a larger realm. Now the larger cigarette companies were going to come up with filter brands of their own. In fact, they already had. Brown & Williamson had introduced filtered Viceroys at a popular price in 1936; they outsold Parliament.

If smallish Lorillard's Kent and B&W's Viceroy could take market share from Parliament, what would happen when the heavyweights entered the arena? Their filter brands would be heavily promoted and advertised, and probably ultimately sell for the same price as regulars or a few cents more. We would have to compete against these companies. How could Benson & Hedges survive such a contest? Most important, we really did not have a competitive filter in Parliament. The filter was made of cotton, and while it did remove some tar and nicotine, it was not what most people would call a real filter.

Dad thought Parliament was simply a more attractively packaged product than the others, and he was right on this score. But it was the filter that created sales. B&H simply didn't have the resources to compete in the raw material, production, and marketing. Either we had to come up with a better filter and a less costly package or we had to consider selling the company before it was overwhelmed by the big firms.

I talked matters over with my brother Edgar, who agreed with me, and we tried to talk Dad into seeking a buyer for the company. He was adamant in rejecting the idea. He had come to love B&H, and did not want to alter things there. But Edgar and I thought he might change his mind if the right offer came from the right person. We both agreed that that person was Al Lyon, an old friend of the family who had risen to become chairman at Philip Morris. Dad and Al were close friends, and Edgar knew Al, too; so we decided Edgar was the person to make the contact.

Soon after Edgar and Al flew back to New York from the Bahamas, Edgar raised the issue. At the time Philip Morris was not the company it is today, but along with Liggett, Brown & Williamson, and Lorillard was part of the group of mid-sized companies behind American Tobacco and R. J. Reynolds. PM could not hope to match American Tobacco or RJR in research funding, but it could get a head start by taking over an already existing name in filtered smoking, Parliament.

Lyon saw the logic, and told Edgar, "Tell your father to give me a call." Now we went to work on Dad, and soon had the impression that while he still wanted to hang on to B&H, he would sell at the right price. Dad could never resist a good deal.

Negotiations began soon after, and in late 1953 Tobacco and Allied agreed to sell to PM its major holding in B&H for $22.4 million in PM stock, 367,829 shares in all. Almost all the B&H shareholders accepted the PM offer. This was twenty-five times earnings, more than twice what the industry leaders' stocks were selling at. The other stockholders, who owned only a small percentage of B&H, came in later. The agreement was approved in April 1954 at a PM stockholders' meeting in Richmond.

Many within the industry thought PM had paid too much for B&H. PM stock declined on the news, while B&H shot up. One publication noted that PM was paying $22.4 million for control of a company whose total assets came to $5.9 million. "$16 million for a name" is the way *Forbes* put it.

Al Lyon would have disagreed. PM was getting great future trademarks and a good name, Parliament, that of the brand leader in the small premium filter field. He was also obtaining the machines capable of turning out quality filter cigarettes, and this counted for something. The B&H labor force was no small matter, either. In addition, he was getting some management talent lacking at PM. Cliff Goldsmith was one of the best people in operations, and soon after the sale he was put in charge of the new PM reconstituted-leaf program—a process for converting short pieces of tobacco into usable tobacco sheet—which turned out to be extremely important not only to PM, but to the entire industry. Then there was my cousin Hugh Cullman, who was also a fine manager. My work with Parliament had won me notice within the industry as well.

My father knew more about tobacco and the industry than many people in the business and he became chairman of the PM executive committee. He died less than a year later, on March 18, 1955, but he'd finally had a taste of the big time, which he enjoyed. He thought about the business to the very end. On his deathbed he told me that PM's popular English Blend, our biggest seller, was flawed—it had too many stems.

Even before the B&H people migrated to the Philip Morris building at 100 Park Avenue, we were aware that we were not only going at the right time but to the right company. PM was not an industry colossus. In 1953 the "big two," American Tobacco and R. J. Reynolds, had revenues of more than $1 billion and $881 million respectively. PM's revenues that year were $315 million—respectable, but not threatening. It would have been a mistake for B&H to have been taken over by one of the larger companies, in part because as a minor part of a giant enterprise we would have been shunted off to a corner, and because these were family dominated companies.

The ghosts of Percival Hill and George Washington Hill hovered over American Tobacco, and for a while George Junior seemed in line for succession. As it happened, Vincent Riggio, who once had been Hill's personal barber, followed Hill, to be succeeded by the smooth and able Paul Hahn. So there would be no Hill dynasty, but the clannish trappings remained. American Tobacco's culture dictated moves up the ladder by insiders; in this period it appeared no outsider could hope for much there.

A similar situation existed at R. J. Reynolds—the name told it all. Dick Reynolds had put his stamp on the company, it was enhanced by the respected Bowman Gray, and there it remained. It was a southern firm, more specifically North Carolinian. The headquarters were in Winston-Salem, and it was only natural for this company to name two cigarettes after its hometown.

In contrast, Philip Morris was deemed an upstart, a New York concern ruled by people who had little connection with Virginia or North Carolina, the homeland of tobacco. Al Lyon was an Englishman who had been in the international cigarette business, and loved to tell stories about his travels to exotic places. Fluent in six languages, he moved easily among the business elite, but the narrow cigarette people considered him an outsider.

PM's president, Oliver Parker McComas, was even more of an outsider in the tobacco world. When he arrived in 1946 PM's earnings were down, and it seemed more bad times were in prospect. With the company in shaky financial shape and in ill favor on Wall Street due to oversights in reporting, Lyon felt he needed a financial person to give the company credibility. In came McComas, who at the time was a vice president at the Paris office of Bankers Trust, which handled the Philip Morris account. Although McComas came from a family that grew tobacco in Maryland, he never claimed to be a tobacco man. But within a year he had been named executive vice president of Philip Morris and then moved up to the presidency. That sort of move couldn't have happened at American Tobacco or R. J. Reynolds.

Milton Biow, whose small New York advertising firm was the longtime agency for Philip Morris, was a brilliant marketer. He was the man responsible for one of the great marketing symbols in cigarette history: Johnny Roventini. Roventini, a forty-three-inch Brooklynite became "Johnny the pageboy," who said, "Call for Philip Morris," in radio ads and appeared in many print ads as well. Milton Biow first heard Johnny Roventini's piercing page in the lobby of the New Yorker Hotel. Johnny is still alive and well in his eighties.

Parker McComas and the PM team had done a fine job. By 1950 the company posted revenues of $256 million, up from $179 million in 1946, and an operating profit of $27 million versus $8 million in 1946. It was then the fourth-largest cigarette company, closing in on Liggett & Myers with Chesterfield, which was in third position. McComas moved the company from its cramped and dingy offices on lower Park Avenue near Eighteenth Street to three floors in the more elegant 100 Park Avenue, within a stone's throw of Grand Central Station, an easy commute for those Philip Morris people who lived in Westchester County and Connecticut.

The growth at PM did not last, however, and by the time we arrived at PM in 1954 there were weaknesses in power and expertise at the top. Lyon was around seventy then, while McComas hadn't really developed a feel for the product line, which was aging and stagnant. The principal brand, Philip Morris English Blend in a brown pack, had not been growing. For a while McComas had some hope for Dunhill, a king-sized filter cigarette, but Dunhill was not a winner. In 1954 he tried to make a go of a king-sized Philip Morris—not a big winner.

But there was hope, in part because PM was willing to bring in outside people and reward them for performance. One of these was Robert Roper, an energetic Richmond native who came in to take charge of personnel and operations. PM also hired Ross Millhiser, who had been captured twice during the war and escaped both times. I thought that anyone who could do that shouldn't have trouble with business. He was a Yale man, who had positive ideas on almost any subject. Millhiser knew Roper and wound up in marketing.

For public relations, McComas put the Benjamin Sonnenberg firm on retainer. With Sonnenberg came George Weissman, a young man who had been raised in the Bronx and attended City College of New York. Weissman found that he could make more money as a newspaperman than an accountant, so he took that route. He bounced from job to job, served as skipper of a submarine chaser during World War II, and after being discharged went back to writing, not only for newspapers but also for a motion picture studio, where he did PR work. This led him to Sonnenberg. Weissman was assigned to the PM account. All these people were there when I arrived.

Jack Landry was another important young person at PM. He was a tall, good-looking guy, and a football fanatic. Jack was a great friend of National Football League Com-

The original Marlboro Man, January 1955.

All part of the Marlboro saga, with Wirt Hatcher of Richmond Recipe fame and Jim Covington of Universal Leaf.

"New from Philip Morris. . ."

With José Cordido-Freytes *(middle)*, our first non-American board member in Caracas.

Receiving the one-hundred-billionth Marlboro from Andrew Britten, May 31, 1960.

The Marlboro machine rolls on.

Under Secretary of Commerce Franklin Delano Roosevelt Jr. presents me with an export award in 1963.

Entering the Tobacco
Hall of Fame, 1962.

*From left to right:* Jack Kopp and Cap Adams of the Leo Burnett team, with
Marboro stalwart Jack Landry and me.

Whitney Young, president of the Urban League, with Henry Ford and me.

Margaret Young, Whitney's widow, was the first woman member of our board. Here she attends a dinner for the Whitney Young Memorial Foundation. The incomparable Leontyne Price is to the right.

I've been visiting FTR since 1964. This is a photo of an early visit.

With Governor Hugh Carey at the time of my appointment as Commissioner of the Port Authority of New York and New Jersey.

Elvis Presley and I sing the Profit Sharing Song, Louisville, 1956.

An ad for the original Parliament in its elegant crush-proof box, early 1950s.

The new Parliament appeared in a flip-top box at a lower price in the late 1950s.

During the same decade, PM shifted from a brown box to red and white.

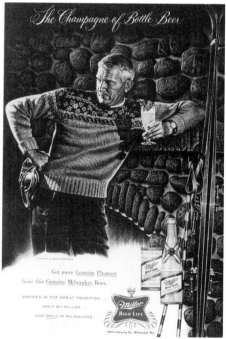

An early Miller High Life ad.

Oh, the disadvantages!

Twenty years after the first ads, Marlboro country is an established idea.

Playing tennis at Forest Hills.

missioner Pete Rozelle and knew many players. He was raised around horses in Saratoga, New York, which was where his interest in sports developed. After bouncing from place to place for a while, he wound up in advertising for a coal company. His job was to convince customers that his coal was superior, a tough sell to say the least. His interest in sports and advertising led to PM, where he was put in promotion. We became the first sponsor on CBS of National Football League games, and I felt very good about that.

It wasn't long before I discovered that some of the people at Philip Morris were working to revive an old PM brand, Marlboro, which had come out in 1924. Back in the twenties it had been the idea of Reuben Ellis, then the president of Philip Morris. Ellis introduced Marlboro as a premium-priced cigarette (ten cents a pack more than regular brands) aimed at those women who in the aftermath of World War I had taken to smoking.

To differentiate the brand further, in 1930 Marlboro was given an ivory-colored tip to keep the cigarette paper from sticking to the woman smoker's lips. It was sold in a white pack bearing a black royal crest with "Philip Morris" in script across the front. The key word in the ads was "mild."

At first sales weren't particularly impressive. By the early 1930s, however, Marlboro was the most popular brand in the PM stable, more profitable than Paul Jones, the company's ten-cent brand, which had also been introduced in 1930. But demand for premium anything was low during the Great Depression. PM struggled through the tough years; earnings rose toward the end of the 1930s, but then hit a plateau.

In the early 1950s, Weissman, who had risen to become McComas's executive assistant, wrote a memo containing two major recommendations. The first dealt with the matter of corporate structure. Stated simply, there wasn't much of it. More money had to be allocated to research, and to obtaining accurate statistics, and the flow of information had to be regularized. In other words, PM had to shape up.

The second point concerned the product line. Lorillard was doing very well with Kent, a filter brand, wrote Weissman, and he was impressed by Parliament's sales. Of course I knew nothing of this at the time, but it was that memo that motivated Lyon and McComas to come after my father's company, Benson & Hedges. The industry's future rested with filters like Kent and Parliament. PM had to take risks, introduce new products, learn more about the market.

Regarding the first matter, that of structure, Weissman's critique obliged McComas to give the matter more thought. When Philip Morris was a small company, in the 1930s and 1940s, it was possible to run it by the seat of the pants. All of the company's executives were in the same three floors and saw each other every day. McComas knew the people's strengths and weaknesses. If a problem or idea arose, he could walk down the hall or take the elevator to the proper floor, stroll into an office, and have a talk with whoever was to be given the new assignment.

But by the time Weissman wrote his memo, too much was happening too quickly for this to work. Delegation of authority and responsibility was needed, and this became even more obvious once Marlboro took off. So, in 1955, McComas established a brand manager system. Millhiser was to carry the ball for Marlboro, Hugh Cullman for Parliament, and John Latham for Philip Morris.

On the second point Weissman and Millhiser asked the Elmo Roper polling organization to help them decide what to do next insofar as product line was concerned. An army of Roper people interviewed 10,000 smokers to discover their preferences. The results were quite revealing. Most of the respondents had given filters a trial; three out of five didn't like them and went back to the unfiltered brands. They didn't like the taste, and the males considered them effeminate.

As I said, Kent was going great guns in the middle and late 1950s, but soon sales leveled off and then they eventually declined. The smokers seemed to like the idea of a filtered smoke, but—as the Roper interviewees indicated—they didn't like the taste of those on the market. This was critical as far as Weissman, Millhiser, and McComas were concerned. PM had a chance to crack this market, perhaps in a big way. What was needed was a full-flavored filter brand that had a virile image.

Impressed with Weissman's efforts, McComas made him vice president in charge of marketing, packaging, and new products. A problem was that Weissman wasn't a tobacco man and was still learning the ropes after less than a year at the firm. But he did a fine job, taking on consultants and testing laboratories, roaming the company, seeking talent, going outside for it when necessary.

Early on, it was agreed the new cigarette would be called Marlboro. The cigarette had a quality image, and brand familiarity would give it a head start in the market, reducing introductory advertising and promotional costs. Moreover, except for one country, Canada, Philip Morris had world rights to the name, and this was to prove extremely important. This use of Marlboro was not my idea. Weissman was key in all this and would remain a critical ingredient for us in the years that followed.

While PM continued to explore the matters of consumer desires and image, Clark Ames, PM's production man in Richmond, came across a radically different kind of package, the flip-top box used in England. It was manufactured by new high-speed machines made by Molins, a top company in a small industry. As smokers know, the basic American soft pack has three rows of cigarettes, staggered in lines of seven, six, and seven. The new flip-top package had two rows of ten cigarettes each. The pack was made of cardboard and so was crushproof. It was only a fraction larger than the standard American pack, which meant it could fit into existing vending machines and into shirt pockets. The cigarette was 80 millimeters long, longer than regular 70s, shorter than 85s.

Within the industry there is a saying that "No one smokes the package." But the appearance, feel, weight, size, and durability of cigarette packages have been demonstrated to be factors in preference and sales. The package was to be important in creating that image that PM was working on. The new red and white Marlboro flip-top box certainly looked classy.

Let me expand a little on the importance of Marlboro packaging. During the years that followed the reformulation and launch of Marlboro, we came out with several variations of the brand. The most important was Marlboro Lights, introduced in 1972, which today outsell the original Marlboro red. In each instance we produced a variant of the original package design, so that smokers would instantly recognize that they had gone from one member of the family, as it were, to another. Over time, we would change some of our other brands' packages drastically, the most important being Parliament, which was reintroduced as a high-filtration popular priced cigarette in flip-top and soft pack in 1958, and has a completely different appearance today from what it was when B&H became part of PM.*

*I should note here that such alteration is unusual but not unheard of. Before World War II the Lucky Strike green package was also very identifiable. But George Washington Hill felt it was a drawback in the contest against Camel and Chesterfield, which were clean and white, and Philip Morris's warm brown. When the United States entered the war, Hill switched to a white pack, advertising that "Lucky Strike Green Has Gone to War." The public was supposed to think that American Tobacco had

Back to 1954 and the development of the new Marlboro. The next step was to tackle the problem of the new packaging. Philip Morris commissioned Frank Gianninoto & Associates, a design firm, to develop the design for the new pack, including cartons and point-of-sales ads. The Color Research Institute of Chicago was called in to design the color layout, and cooperated with Gianninoto in running mechanical tests.

The package design that emerged after much study was red and white, with a row of stripes in the upper section. The bottom part of the package was white, and the design started tapering at midpoint, where the red came in. The name itself was in lowercase letters to make it appear different and stylized. The PM crest was also included. I wasn't too happy with this look, because to me it seemed different just for the sake of being different. We had packages designed for various test products: a standard 85-millimeter filter cigarette in a soft pack; an 85-millimeter nonfilter cigarette in a soft pack; an 80-millimeter cigarette with a flush filter in a flip-top box; and an 80-millimeter cigarette with a recessed filter, also in a flip-top box.

I suppose describing the packaging really isn't necessary, even though the design was changed somewhat in development. Is there anyone who has not seen the Marlboro package? Is it necessary to describe the Coca-Cola bottle or logo, or the McDonald's arches? The Marlboro pack is in that league today.

Others at PM were considering the product itself, and

gotten rid of the green pack for reasons of patriotism, that the green ink would be used for camouflage. This simply wasn't the case. Then he switched to another slogan: "L.S./M.F.T.—Lucky Strike Means Fine Tobacco," in which the initials sounded like a code signal, this being considered appropriate in wartime. So the package and slogan were and are important marketing devices.

here some Benson & Hedges people came in. McComas wanted our company for Parliament, but he also knew he could use some experienced tobacco and cigarette-making personnel. By acquiring B&H, McComas would be getting a team of veterans who could help. But PM had the premier tobacco man in the U.S. industry in Wirt Hatcher of Richmond, Virginia. Hatcher later developed the "Richmond recipe" blend for Marlboro, a critical factor in the brand's success.

Such was the situation as I found it when we took that short trip to PM's Park Avenue offices in early 1954. We were to join the Marlboro team. I was to be a vice president in marketing; as McComas told me soon after I arrived, "Your job is going to be to develop a popular-priced filter cigarette for Philip Morris, called Marlboro." The job included the test-marketing of four different Marlboros and the product development that by then was under way.

From the first we knew the Parliament cotton filter wouldn't do. Kent had a "micronite" filter. Some of the new brands of 1953–1954 had cellulose filters. L&M advertised the "Pure White Miracle Tip of Alpha-Cellulose." Tareyton used cellulose too, plus a bit of activated charcoal. It was a time for experimentation.

Our Marlboro filter, too, was composed of cellulose acetate, which we called "Selectrate." It was developed after years of research. In its final form the filter was something like a miniature humidor. Each filter contained filaments of special acetate. It was unique, and we thought it an improvement over then-existing filters.

Now for the tobacco blend. By then R. J. Reynolds had introduced Winston, which seemed to provide improved taste in a filter product. Winston came out in the spring of 1954 and sold 7.5 billion units in its first year, making it the thirteenth-best seller in the entire industry and one of the top performers in its segment. It rose to fifth place in 1955, with

23 billion units. To come up with a better blend than Winston's was the task of PM's veteran leaf specialist and blender, Wirt Hargrove Hatcher, who had created the blend for the old premium Marlboro.

The old Marlboro had been based mostly on Virginia bright leaf (i.e., flue cured), which was one of the earliest tobaccos used in cigarettes. The new Marlboro had Virginia and burley. Burley had an ability to absorb flavorings. We added a small amount of Turkish and Oriental leaf and flavoring. Hatcher experimented with several blends, and finally came up with a blend a PM panel decided was just right, which he called the Richmond recipe.

Its taste was richer than Winston's, and at the same time smoother. We spared no expense in the blend, which we considered the class of the field. Then we conducted blind tests pitting Marlboro against Winston, and we always came out ahead by two to one. So we knew we had a better product—a superior blend—and we made the cigarette awfully well.

We now had the blend, the filter, and several different packages in place. But several choices had to be made before we could start test-marketing. One was the color of the tip. Should it be white or cork? Should the filter be recessed, as it was in Parliament, or flush, as with the new filter cigarettes? These may seem unimportant and arcane matters, but we agonized over such questions for days. Some argued that the white tip would appeal to health-conscious smokers, the kind who were taking to filters, while the cork tip would seem more rugged to the male smokers for whom Marlboro was being repositioned.

We decided to test-market various combinations: Marlboro 85 in a soft pack, with acetate flush filter and nonfilter; and Marlboro 80 in the flip-top box, flush and recessed filter. We chose four markets—Dallas, Denver, Providence, and Rochester. I went to all four to see what the public's reaction was. We thought this was an important step. We wanted to be right. I think this market testing was one of the best things we ever did. We were testing a new flip-top box, which was very creative packaging, the first packaging change to occur since about 1918—almost forty years. We wanted to test which would be the best Marlboro filter. So we tested the filter, the blend, the product, and the packaging, to come up with the right answer. Getting answers on packaging was a complicated and tricky operation. We tested the pack for eye appeal, readability, and identification. Hidden cameras activated by photoelectric cells, one-way mirrors, ocular measurement, and other devices were used to check customer reactions.

After years of research involving twenty-seven PM executives and supervisors alone, plus twenty-five scientists and technicians, eight outside consultants, six independent laboratories, one research organization, and scores of PM employees, we had our product. From these tests we concluded that the flush filter cork-tipped version, which was tested in Dallas, was preferred to the others.

I telephoned Parker McComas from Dallas and told him, "The reaction to the packaging is sensational, and forget about conducting more research—they want the flush filter."

McComas answered, "Joe, I have to make a big and expensive decision. We can have an exclusive on the flip-top box for two years if we give Molins enough orders to keep them busy for that long."

I thought about it for a little while, and then I said, "Parker, place the order." There was no question in my mind that we had a very exciting new packaging idea. We placed the order with Molins, so we were there with this new, revolutionary package—and we'd have at least a two-year lead on the competition in the United States.

Now, with all our ducks lined up, we had to locate the proper field general for the advertising campaign. We considered many of the large, small, and mid-sized agencies located within a stroll of our Park Avenue offices. We were not impressed by any of them. Till then, cigarette companies had looked to eastern agencies for campaigns. We wanted to do something quite radical for the times. Ross Millhiser urged me to consider Leo Burnett, a small Chicago outfit that had been founded in 1935, whose greatest triumph so far had been the Jolly Green Giant, for the Minnesota Valley Canning Company, and Kellogg cereals. In time Burnett would be recognized as a genius in his field, creating the Pillsbury Doughboy and the Keebler elves, but in 1954 he was simply one of the bunch.

We sent him samples of what products and packaging we had, and gave him a few days. Then Roger Green, who was our advertising manager, and I traveled to Chicago on the Twentieth Century Limited train to meet with the man in whose hands we might be placing our future.

Burnett was a stocky man with bushy eyebrows and a froglike face, large lips, and puffy cheeks, but a very nice smile. He was decisive, with a strong personality, very creative, and rather soft-spoken, with a husky voice. Unlike many of the New York ad men, he had nothing slick about him. Maybe there is something to the notion of midwestern honesty, integrity, and directness; Burnett possessed these qualities in spades. The New York advertising people might have been fine for a cigarette like Parliament or Virginia Rounds. In Marlboro we wanted a blockbuster for the entire nation. Burnett seemed the best person to deliver for us this time. In those days, agencies were headed by their creative people—David Ogilvy of Ogilvy & Mather, Mary Wells of Wells, Rich, Greene, Bill Bernbach of DD&B, and in Chicago, Leo Burnett of the Leo Burnett agency.

Leo Burnett was a cigarette smoker, and immediately told us we had a fine product. I put the new package on his desk and he sort of looked at it. I remember that he shook his head a little, while we told him we wanted this to be a popular-priced cigarette that would appeal to all age groups and both sexes throughout the country.

We went over the history of Marlboro, and I added that it had been a premium-priced woman's cigarette but we wanted to change the image significantly. We were at it for about two hours and then he said he wanted to think overnight about Marlboro, and asked whether we could come to the office the following morning. We could and did; we were there at 9:00 A.M.

Leo Burnett and his art director were there to greet us. He came to the point very quickly. Burnett didn't like the lowercase "M" in "Marlboro" on the box, which he felt was a turnoff. And the stripes on the red "roof" of the box gave it a busy look that was not at all classy, so he had changed it to a solid red. He liked the flip-top box, although he doubted smokers would buy the cigarette for that alone. Still, he wanted to feature it in his ads. His art director had changed the design to the solid red "roof" on the flip-top box.

The first ad Burnett showed us had that box all right, but most of the picture was of a cowboy. He explained to us that we wanted our cigarette to have a masculine image, and there was nothing more masculine in America than the weatherbeaten, mythic cowboy, conveying a certain gritty honesty and flavor. He had considered other symbols but rejected them all. One was a New York cabbie, but such a symbol would connote an urban smoke. Cowboys appealed to all classes in all parts of the country. I liked the cowboy image the minute Burnett showed it to us.

Then he came up with the slogan: "New from Philip Morris. You get a lot to like—filter, flavor, flip-top box."

Burnett explained it to us: "Here is what we are going to say—'New from Philip Morris,' because we want people to know that Marlboro is made by a credible, recognized manufacturer. The newness makes it exciting, and we go on to describe it: 'You get a lot to like—filter, flavor, flip-top box.'" He concluded that the cowboy was the right image, not only for men, but also for women.

Roger Green and I took the ad back to New York on the train. We showed it to Landry, Weissman, Millhiser, McComas, and the others; everyone was impressed. All this happened in December 1954.

With this we went into the manufacturing phase, at first with our first Molins packers in our Stockton Street factory in Richmond, which geared up to produce the new Marlboros. For a while everything seemed to conspire against us. The Molins packers broke down. The Marlboro boxes were absorbing moisture from the cigarette tobacco and felt clammy. It was a tough period for the company, since both revenues and profits had declined in 1954. PM, which once had ambitions of becoming the third-largest factor in the industry, was now fifth and falling. I don't want to be too dramatic about this, but in those days Marlboro was a make-or-break product for Philip Morris.

Marlboro was introduced in New York in January 1955, with just that first "New from Philip Morris" print advertisement. We had nothing else—no radio or television. It was an instant success. Within one month Marlboro was the number-one brand in the greater New York metropolitan area.

In 1954 we had sold some 300 million units of the old premium Marlboro. In 1955 we sold 6.7 billion Marlboros, and we would have sold more if only the Stockton Street factory could have turned them out. As it was, our facilities were operating seven days a week, twenty-four hours a day, and we still couldn't meet demand. We flew in new machines from England and installed them as quickly as possible; still, the demand could not be satisfied. PM had to allocate Marlboros to our wholesalers for three years. This kind of acceptance was most unusual. In order to come close to it, one has to go back to the arrival of Camel in 1913–1914. PM revenues went from $282 million in 1954 to $327 million in 1956, while earnings rose from $11.3 million to $12.7 million. We crossed the $500 million sales mark handily in 1960, a year in which earnings were $21 million. Our common stock, languishing around 40 when Marlboro was introduced, didn't perform much better until 1958, because Wall Street didn't believe the cigarette's popularity would last. They must have thought Marlboro would fizzle out the way Kent had. It didn't happen, and now the stock soared, reaching 80 by the end of 1960 and rising to more than 120 the following year. One hardly expected this kind of action from a tobacco stock, or the many splits that followed.

Subsequent Burnett print, radio, and TV ads were catchy and appealing. We used the cowboy, but also introduced other symbolic figures: the businessman; the naval officer; the golfer. Sometimes he had a tattoo on the back of his hand. In the process, what had begun life as a woman's brand metamorphosed into a man's. Interestingly enough, we won many women smokers as well.

I'm not suggesting we had unalloyed successes in this period. There were the inevitable setbacks. One of these came when the Marlboro success was still questionable, in 1955.

The national introduction of Marlboro coincided with far more important events: the May 1954 Supreme Court order to desegregate public schools and the Interstate Commerce Commission's November 1955 ban on segregation in interstate transportation. This set off a firestorm of opposition in much of the white South. Any individual or company associated even indirectly with the civil rights movement was bound to suffer consequences at the hands of extremists in that section of the country.

More than most companies, Philip Morris had attempted

to reach out in this area. We had made contributions to the National Urban League, a prominent Black civil rights organization. Our Richmond facilities were more integrated than any other in the industry. We had a Black sales executive and were about to hire more. As I've already mentioned, we were perceived as a New York, not a southern, tobacco company. There were several Jews, I among them, in visible positions. In this period, when Jews were prominent in the civil rights struggle and segments of the white South identified Jews as radicals, troublemakers, and—let's not be afraid to use the word—"nigger lovers" (this was more than four decades ago) Philip Morris was, unsurprisingly, singled out for retribution.

Those who opposed our integration policies and support distributed copies of a picture of me handing Lester Granger, then head of the national Urban League, a check for $1,000. This produced a boycott of PM brands throughout the South, from Marlboro on down. Company cars had their tires slashed; our reps were turned away by old customers. Reps would drive into service stations to gas up, and when the man at the pump saw that Philip Morris logo, he would turn away.

Let me reiterate that at the time we were rationing Marlboros to our distributors; our aggregate sales were not affected by the boycott. Philip Morris endured boycotts as well as personal attacks on its people and property because it would not give in to this bigotry. Parker McComas and the rest of us did what we thought was the right thing, and we had to bear the consequences of our actions.

All the while Burnett kept on churning out new ads. One 1963 TV ad showed an empty football stadium into which a cowboy stepped and said, "This is Marlboro Country." Marlboro Country is everywhere, he meant. Singer Julie London, a very sultry lady with a silky voice, sang "Where there's a man there's a Marlboro," and that original Burnett theme, "You get a lot to like with a Marlboro—filter, flavor, flip-top box." Jackie Gleason, then the top-rated TV personality, would take a drag on a Marlboro, and utter his trademark statement: "How sweet it is!"

Then a member of the Burnett team came up with a real winner. He came to us with film for a Marlboro TV ad with background music—the Elmer Bernstein *Magnificent Seven* theme, which was very exciting music, evocative of the cowboy life and the American West. All of us were immediately taken with what Burnett's people had produced for us. We purchased the rights to the music from United Artists. Many people still remember those Marlboro Country ads with Bernstein's *Magnificent Seven* score. Whenever I see a Marlboro ad that great theme comes to mind.

Permit me to end this section on the introduction of Marlboro by noting that in 1963 we were still the smallest of the major cigarette companies. But we felt we had a smoother, richer cigarette than any of the competition, including the industry leader, Winston. It would take years to get Marlboro to its world-leadership position. This was truly a campaign, not a one-shot introduction.

# CHAPTER FOUR

# *Abroad*

*It is time for a new generation of leadership, to cope with new problems, and new opportunities. For there is a new world to be won.*

—John F. Kennedy
July 4, 1960

LIFE CAN BE VERY SIMPLE in small companies. With my help, Dad was able to run Benson & Hedges out of his hip pocket. He knew most aspects of the business, from leaf buying to production to distribution. I handled marketing and advertising, but he was always there, checking on what was happening. He didn't have to worry about fighting government regulations; he simply obeyed them without much question. B&H did not engage in lobbying and did not have to concern itself with markets outside of the United States or with diversification. Dad never had to consider brand extensions; I wonder what he would have thought had someone suggested the introduction of Parliament Lights or Parliament Menthols. If B&H had been an independent company when the health issue first appeared, Dad probably would have remained quiet, permitting the heavy hitters to take the lead in this area.

Philip Morris was an entirely different kind of company,

but still no giant, when I arrived in 1954. It was modest compared to what it had become by the time I stepped down as CEO in 1978. In the 1950s PM's horizon and possibilities were limited, but then they expanded greatly as the business grew. Soon I would have to deal with a variety of concerns Dad could only have imagined. For him, B&H was a part-time job. He would spend a few hours a day there, and some at Cullman Brothers, which he also ran. In small companies the CEO must be a tactician as well as a strategist. Dad would have been amazed at how much of the work at PM was delegated to others.

I tried to be surrounded by talented, aggressive, experienced people. I hoped each of them harbored thoughts that they could have done my job better than I. Modesty and diffidence are fine qualities, but the top posts at companies like Philip Morris require a measure of self-confidence and aggression. These are the people who execute policy, and who, if successful, get into positions where they dictate strategy. The path to the top at PM after I arrived went through the ranks. All of the CEOs since me have taken this route.

And one of the most important parts of the route to the top lay in the international arena, which was one of the areas where I was most active. We were a minor industry force in the United States until Marlboro. In 1975, twenty years after Marlboro was introduced, PM had 25 percent of domestic sales, behind RJR, which had a 33 percent market share. By then, however, we were the largest company in the world in unit volume as a result of our international sales, which accounted for 20 percent of our business—up from nothing when I came through the door.

Today Marlboro is, in all its forms, the leading packaged consumer product in the world. But most people outside the industry may not realize that PM is truly a global packaged consumer goods company, not just a tobacco company. It is true that our international cigarette revenues are significant; in fact they are twice as large as those in the United States, and for these reasons, PM is considered a tobacco company. But we get almost as much revenue from food and beer as from tobacco; Philip Morris is the country's largest food company and is second in the world, behind Nestlé.

I stress here that we made the move overseas and entered into our first steps of diversification simultaneously. Both of these developments, as did the origins of Marlboro, started with CEO Parker McComas, but he was unable to see them through, so I should tell you how I became McComas' successor.

It happened very suddenly. In the autumn of 1957 McComas, who was then sixty-two years old, learned he had cancer. The prognosis was guarded, and his doctor recommended exploratory surgery. All of us knew this was a very serious matter. If all went well, McComas might come out of the experience a healthy man. If the cancer was too far gone, then he would most likely retire and deal with his illness, a personal tragedy but a situation that would allow PM some time to adjust to and prepare for succession. The operation took place in late November at New York's Lenox Hill Hospital; he suffered a heart attack after the surgery and died.

McComas was an important figure in PM history. He was intelligent; he had a vision and created the organization to carry it out. In November 1957, the PM board was faced with the immediate problem of choosing a successor, something that hadn't occupied their thoughts before that sudden death. As executive vice president I was the leading candidate, but was by no means a shoo-in. I hadn't been at PM that long, and while I had earned the respect of the board for leading the Marlboro introduction, at the age of forty-five I was considered by some simply too young for the job. So the board took several months to think about me and look outside the firm for a possible McComas successor. In the end I got the job, at first as acting CEO for half a year, and then as CEO in all respects. So I picked up the reins McComas had bequeathed me, including the overseas expansion he had begun.

The domestic success with Marlboro had led us to take this long-overdue step. The American market was large, but the world market was so much bigger. American manufacturers of all sorts of products had been seeking foreign markets, but the cigarette companies held back.

In the early postwar period, national tastes in cigarettes made international cigarette marketing a chancy proposition, to say the least. In the U.K., Virginia flue-cured tobacco without flavoring was preferred, as it was in most other English-speaking countries. Many Continental Europeans preferred dark, air-cured, Virginia leaf cigarettes. Filters were not popular. American cigarettes were novelties, no more than that. No one even considered marketing American cigarettes in the Communist bloc or in Asia. Buying them in Paris was as difficult as purchasing Gauloises and Gitanes in New York. If you don't recognize the names of these French dark blend cigarettes, you'll know what I mean.

Even had the American companies been able to overcome the differences in tastes and tradition, there were other formidable obstacles. While many countries considered themselves bastions of free enterprise, that wasn't the case with respect to tobacco: state monopolies ruled. This was the situation in such western countries as France, Spain, and Italy, as well as Japan.

We were free to export our products to these countries, but the tariffs, excises, and other obstacles were onerous. Suppose an American firm could surmount all these drawbacks, and foreign demand was such that smokers were willing to pay extra for Marlboros, Winstons, and the rest. What then? Many countries had regulations requiring that cigarettes be made at least partly with domestically grown leaf.

Some of them required that the subsidiary producing the cigarettes be partially or completely owned by their own nationals.

Finally, there was the British American Tobacco problem. At the turn of the century, American Tobacco's "Buck" Duke had invaded the British market with his cigarettes, and the firms there reacted by organizing Imperial Tobacco to meet the American challenge. A major price war followed, in which both interests were hurt. In the end they came to an agreement which, in effect, divided the world into two segments. Duke sold his British company to Imperial Tobacco, which would use it for U.K. sales, and organized British American Tobacco, or "BAT," with Duke receiving two-thirds of the stock and becoming chairman of the board. BAT was designated to sell Imperial and American brands everywhere in the world outside the United Kingdom. Under the terms of the agreement, much amended over the years, BAT did not own its brands in the U.K. but did own Brown & Williamson in the United States and was a presence in all other markets; at this time, in fact, BAT was the world's largest cigarette company not controlled by governments.

Even taking all these factors into consideration, there should have been an American attempt to go international before we made the move. What made the situation stranger still was the great popularity American cigarettes had enjoyed overseas during World War II. Our soldiers took them wherever they went, and shared the smokes with Allied soldiers and civilians in Europe and the Pacific. I had seen this situation while serving in the Navy, and it surprised and intrigued me. I later learned that in the early days of the occupations in Europe and Asia, our cigarettes were used as currency—but only American brands, no others. American cigarettes were *preferred* to money.

There were both good and bad reasons for individual

American tobacco companies not having gone overseas. The good reasons were specific business constraints. For example, the U.S. company Brown & Williamson was a wholly-owned subsidiary of BAT, and the parent didn't want B&W to invade its world markets. And some of the other companies, like Lorillard, were too small to market their products in other parts of the world. The bad reason was a narrow view of the market, which had been passed on to some of the veteran leaders by their predecessors. Reynolds, in particular, was wedded to the notion that "foreign" meant anyplace outside North Carolina. L&M wasn't as bad, but some at that company also held to this view. American Tobacco, the industry leader, did not make moves into foreign markets because, outside the U.S., its major brands were owned by BAT.

As I have already noted, McComas had been an international banker, working for Bankers Trust in Paris. He knew the world, and was far more cosmopolitan than his counterparts at the other companies. McComas was willing to move where the others held back, and Philip Morris was large enough to mount what in the beginning would be a fairly modest effort.

He had to start virtually from scratch. The company had a lot to learn in this field, and we made some mistakes in the beginning that would have been avoided only a few years later. This is to say, there was a tuition to be paid in the school of hard knocks that was the international cigarette market. But we also had some great successes in those years.

In 1955 there was only one person in the entire PM organization who had anything to do with foreign markets. That was George Dawson, who was responsible for PM's military sales at American post exchanges and exports from the United States. We needed an executive and organization with more experience than that, and we found the right person in Justus Heymans. Heymans, who was of Dutch origin, came from a very small U.S. company called Tobacco Products Export. He brought to the table a wide knowledge of people and institutions, as well as excellent cigarette business connections all over the world. He was a major factor in enabling us to enter new markets, in Europe and the Far East.

Heymans was a colorful character, an aviator who flew his own planes from the Netherlands to other continents. When Amsterdam was about to fall to the Germans in 1940, he went to the airport, got into his plane, and flew to southern England.

He knew tobacco backward and forward. He had been involved in the tobacco leaf business in the Netherlands, and had purchased leaf from Sumatra and Java, countries he knew very well. PM had a major stake in Tobacco Products Export, which exported U.S.-made cigarettes all over the world, especially the remote parts; that was how Justus had gotten his experience. Eventually we folded Tobacco Products Export into PM International. Justus was a very important man, and putting him in charge of our overseas business was a very important development for PM.

Justus Heymans was one prong of our entry into foreign markets. The second lay in forming alliances in those countries where nationals would run the operation. In effect, they would become our licensees. The contracts would give us control over the blending process, raw materials, and quality control. We would assist in advertising. The licensees would pay us a royalty for our brands that they were manufacturing. We were very careful about that. We were demanding, especially when it came to quality, and would dispatch personnel to the manufacturing sites to maintain our high standards. I think it paid off in the long run for our licensees and for us. The net of it all was the worldwide success of Marlboro.

In the case of our initial entry into Australia in 1955—our first step outside the U.S.—we were approached by two

Australian businessmen, Sir Charles Altson, a colorful, engaging fellow who liked his bottle, and Sir Norman Martin. These two men told us they wanted to start a company, to be called Philip Morris Australia, in Melbourne. McComas figured we couldn't go wrong with this arrangement; Australia might be a good springboard for us into the lucrative Asian market. We also sent one of our marketing people out there to help; he came up with a cartoon character called Puffing Billy in an on-premises display unit to help promote the smokes. The Philip Morris brand was a complete failure.

Another failure was Dunhill, whose trademark we were licensed to use at the time. We introduced the brand in Australia, where it was greeted with complete indifference. No, that's not right. It was absolutely rejected; the Australians called it "Dunghill." Incidentally, we had tried a king-sized Dunhill in the American market earlier, and that failed, too. We were so frugal in those days that we refused to pay its holder, a company called Carreras, the $20,000 annual fee required to retain the trademark for PM, which was unfortunate, because it became valuable later as a competitor owned by Rothmans.

Then there was Marlboro. In Australia, half the tobacco in cigarettes had to be domestically grown. We had a tough time making an acceptable Marlboro with the leaf we found there, and it was difficult maintaining quality control at an operation 12,000 miles from New York. Our Australian founders didn't know anything about cigarettes, so we had to send a team there to conduct an educational campaign as well as reformulate the Marlboro blend. Labor costs proved much higher than we thought they would be.

There was also the problem of competition. Through its subsidiary W. D. & H. O. Wills, BAT was a major presence in Australia, with about 75 percent of the market for its brands—one of which was the leader Benson & Hedges, because our U.S. company didn't own the Australian rights to that nameplate. The result of all those factors was a Marlboro failure, and it took years for us to turn it around.

The situation regarding "B&H" and other nameplates was not unusual. There was a Canadian company called Benson & Hedges (Canada) which had the rights to that name and also to "Parliament." This kind of brand division is quite familiar to those in the industry, but may surprise others. Consider that in 1978, for the bargain price of $108 million, Philip Morris acquired the international business and brands of the Liggett Group, which had such cigarettes as Chesterfield and L&M. At the time the Liggett Group's charcoal filter Lark was the best-selling import in Japan.

The cigarette business for B&H (Canada) was tiny in Canada in those days, and the company was primarily involved with cigars. I met with the owner, Gaston Munic, and after a long discussion we acquired the whole B&H business in Canada—cigars, cigarettes, all trademarks including Parliament, and a dilapidated factory in Montreal's Chinatown—for half a million dollars. So outright purchase of a foreign company, in addition to licensees and partnerships, would be the third method of entering a foreign market.

There was only one country in which we did not own the Marlboro trademark, and that was and is Canada, where an affiliate of BAT owns it. Conversely, BAT makes Players there, but we have the Players trademark for the American market. PM cannot produce Marlboro in Canada, BAT cannot make Players in the United States. For years we have tried to arrange a swap, without success.

Initially, licensees seemed the best way to go about the business of expanding markets overseas. I remember that our then legal adviser, Paul Smith, didn't like the idea of forming alliances with licensees. The best way to go when starting with a licensee was to obtain, as part of the deal, an option to purchase majority control of the licensee sometime down the road. Smith was a strong believer in control.

Instead of licensing, Smith suggested, we should seek true partners. While licensing involved the lowest cost and risk to us, our partners would have more incentive to work hard and succeed, and we would be fairly well remunerated for our efforts. In the process we would learn more about the business and markets in very different countries.

Paul Smith had been in Naval Intelligence during World War II. Upon discharge he joined Conboy, Hewitt, the law firm that had handled PM's legal business since the early 1950s. (In this period the company was so small that it didn't have an in-house lawyer.) Smith was a pudgy, intense, single-minded man, who devoted himself completely to whatever client he happened to represent. Within a few years he considered himself an expert on the legal aspects of the cigarette business. McComas and I respected his opinions in this area. In 1957 McComas talked Smith into coming into PM as its first full-time counsel, with the title of vice president, director, and general counsel. McComas died before Smith came aboard, and I was in charge at the time he arrived. Smith was helpful in the early development of our international business. But he clashed repeatedly with Justus Heymans, who was still actively working on business arrangements for us.

In 1955 PM signed a license agreement with La Suerte Cigar and Cigarette, a large Philippine concern; next came a similar arrangement with Tabacalera Nacional SE, a Panama company. These nibbles were followed the next year by a more important deal in Venezuela, where we already had a good export business that was in danger of being shut down by the government there. Were we to work with a local licensee, this problem would be obviated. PM licensed a small cigarette company, C.A. Tabacalera Nacional of Caracas, to manufacture Philip Morris cigarettes. As part of the deal

Smith arranged for PM to receive an option to purchase up to 51 percent of Tabacalera, exercisable in two steps. He did this because of his mistrust of long-term licensees.

Tabacalera opened a factory in the middle of a tobacco field outside Caracas. The Venezuelan government at the time was eager to have us there, and for a while all went pretty well, though BAT competition there, through its Bigott subsidiary, was tough. Then the government changed, and in came an administration that was less friendly. The Venezuelan operation was marginal at best, and lost money at worst.

At this point the lack of earnings in these small overseas companies was not a problem. Our investment wasn't that large to begin with, and given the domestic profits from Marlboro the goal for us wasn't profits but market penetration.

Smith told me when we started out, "Now, Joe, keep away from Europe. Go to Latin America. That's where the real market is going to be." Well, it wasn't that way for PM then, and it isn't that way now. In time we got 80 percent of the Venezuelan market, but it and other parts of Latin America are nowhere as profitable as Europe.

In 1957 we started manufacturing cigarettes in Switzerland with our new licensee, Fabriques de Tabac Réunies (FTR). This was a prestigious house, Switzerland's second-largest cigarette company, with 20 percent of the country's market. FTR started making Marlboros in Neuchâtel. We received a royalty of 40 cents per 1,000 on our cigarettes FTR manufactured in Switzerland, which is less than a penny a pack. Marlboro was a big hit there, and this success led us into other western European markets.

Soon we introduced Marlboros in France, hoping they would do as well there as they had in Italy. As noted, the French smoked those strong, dark-tobacco blended Gauloises and Gitanes put out by SEITA, the French monopoly. SEITA was willing to sell Marlboros in specially designated shops, but at prices much higher than those charged for domestic brands. To obtain market share we slashed our prices so much that we lost money on every pack sold. We wanted French smokers to at least try Marlboro and Parliament, in the hope that they would be attracted to this new taste. In 1961 PM entered into a licensing agreement with SEITA, which enabled them to manufacture and market Parliament.

By 1960 we knew we had to strengthen our overseas management. I had been running the overseas operations as an ancillary part of the general business. In this period I had to run the United States business, run the acquisition and diversification program, and deal with the assault on cigarettes from their critics. So long as the foreign businesses were small and simple, this could be done. But, while still relatively small, they no longer were simple. In addition, the lack of structure had caused problems that had to be addressed by a single, focused individual. That person had to be a strong manager and a diplomat, able to deal effectively with nationals in all parts of the world. He had to be experienced, forceful, and inspirational, with marketing and financial skills.

George Weissman, who at the time was executive vice president for U.S. marketing and was running the domestic tobacco business, had just gone on a European vacation; on impulse, he had taken along ten cartons of Marlboros. On his return he told me how enthusiastic those Europeans to whom he had given the cigarettes had been about Marlboro. This was most evident in West Germany, where there was a large American presence. Many soldiers smoked Marlboro, having purchased them in their post exchanges, and this intrigued the Germans in the cigarette business.

In 1960 Weissman didn't know what I and others were planning for the foreign business. But it was becoming clear to me that Weissman was the best man to handle things at what was to become Philip Morris Overseas. When I told him of my ideas, Weissman was taken aback. He was as ambitious as anyone else at PM, and wanted to be placed in a highly visible position. Was the foreign business to be a cubbyhole into which were placed executives who couldn't hack it in the home market? I assured him this was not the case. To the contrary, the foreign business would be one of PM's most important growth opportunities, a natural springboard for anyone who could resolve some of its problems.

I could understand Weissman's trepidation about leaving the domestic business. Marlboro had a long way to go in the United States, against some very tough competition. In 1960 the nation's best-selling cigarette was Pall Mall, followed by Camel, Winston, and Lucky Strike. Winston was the leading filter brand; Marlboro was in ninth place, behind L&M. Marlboro's sales were slightly less than a third of Pall Mall's, and less than half of Winston's. The people who could move Marlboro ahead of the competition would be winners, worthy of moving up. But the same would be true of those who helped us conquer the global market, which was many times larger than the domestic. Both Weissman and I were well aware of what faced those who, in order to make Marlboro a world leader, tried to sell an American product to Europeans, Latin Americans, Asians, and Africans. A challenge! And we had to do this with very limited resources.

When Weissman became head of PM Overseas he was handed three matters with which to deal. One was the difficult Benson & Hedges situation in Canada. Another was the Venezuelan operation, which was losing market share. The third was the Australian operation, which was also in trouble.

We turned the Venezuelan problem over to John Murphy. The burly New Yorker was not a tobacco man originally, but rather another lawyer at Conboy, Hewitt. Paul

Smith dispatched Murphy to Caracas in 1961 to work out further amplification of the licensing arrangement and to merge the initial licensee with another company in the hope of creating a stronger entity. While he was there our representative had a heart attack, and Murphy was pressed into service to put the deal together and manage the company.

Murphy stayed on for a few months, did a superb job, and then returned to New York. Soon after, he left Conboy and came to PM as assistant general counsel; he became an important figure in the expansion of PM International and later Miller Brewing. The Venezuelan operation came out with some new cigarettes, Capri and Lido, low-priced brands that did fairly well, in part because of a successful ad campaign, "Pido Lido," which means "Ask for a Lido." In time we got a 90 percent market share in Venezuela.

At the same time we were in negotiations on Marlboro for what seemed a promising deal with Martin Brinkmann, West Germany's third-largest cigarette company, just behind BAT. The Brinkmann deal was for ten years, renewable if both parties agreed. Almost from the first Brinkmann gave us the kind of problems Paul Smith had warned us about. First they told us that the Marlboro blend was wrong for German tastes, that we needed more Oriental tobacco if we wanted to have a success. Then Brinkmann refused to use the cowboy theme in the ads, turning instead to old-fashioned bourgeois scenes that made Marlboro appear just another German smoke. These changes brought only limited success.

It went on that way for ten years, during which Marlboro had about 1 percent of the German market, exactly the minimum required to let Brinkmann keep control of Marlboro under the royalty arrangement. Our royalties were around $600,000 a year in Germany during this period, and had Brinkmann not controlled Marlboro's volume we would have made considerably more. Meanwhile RJR entered the

German market with its own subsidiary, which made strides there with Camel.

I've often wondered why Brinkmann acted as it did. It was tough to deal with them. Surely, after the first few years, the company's leaders must have realized that Marlboro was going to make deep inroads into the German market. It was n their interest to treat us decently. Had Brinkmann mounted a meaningful effort to get past that 1 percent market share, we might have renewed the license, and the company would have made far more profits than it did. But despite all the troubles we had with Brinkmann, I have to concede that they did introduce us to the German market. Today Marlboro is the biggest brand in Germany, but PM built it, not Brinkmann.

Brinkmann was not a good partner. Being a good partner is good business. This is a very simple idea and might sound Pollyannaish, but it is true nonetheless. I wanted PM to be as profitable as possible, but that didn't mean squeezing every nickel out of a deal. In working with others we tried to leave enough on the plate to make the other guy feel we were good partners.

In 1963, Fabriques de Tabac Réunies' Swiss owners and management quarreled, and this enabled PM to make a bid for the company. Since we needed a man who knew his numbers for the transactions, Weissman turned the matter over to Murphy, who brought in a Scots accountant, Ronald Hew Thomson, who had been at Coopers (it was not yet Coopers & Lybrand). Thomson went over the books; on the basis of what he saw there and in the marketplace, he urged us not to pass up the chance to acquire this gem of a company. After some tough negotiations, we acquired all of FTR for PM, paying $12 million. We bought our first cigarette-manufacturing affiliate on the European continent.

When the deal was done, some of the New York people

and I flew to Switzerland for a celebration with our new partners. There was the inevitable culture clash. Swiss businessmen tend to be much more formal and status-conscious than Americans. This was the period when American businessmen and businesswomen were starting to call each other by first names after only a short acquaintance. Their Swiss counterparts wouldn't do this until after many years of working together, if then. In addition, I had invited the Swiss to bring their spouses, something that was not done in Switzerland.

After the meal I tried to deliver a warm and upbeat message. I sketched what I thought would be the international nature of PM, and how it might affect some of those present. "This is the dawn of a new age for FTR and Philip Morris," I said. "All of us are going to participate in a vital and dynamic international operation. Someday I'll be seeing some of you working elsewhere in Europe, or elsewhere in the world or at our New York offices, because you are good managers, and good managers can function in any position and place."

As I sat down, I didn't think I'd made much of a dent in their reserve, but I was wrong. Some of our New York people got friendly with their new Swiss co-workers, and tried to spell out what PM ownership entailed. It meant that positions of importance all over the world would be open to talent, not given out on the basis of birth or connections. These were educated people. They had read about American business practices and had met Americans. But now they were on the inside, not outside looking in. And this would make some of them millionaires—in dollars, not in Swiss francs. As the liquor flowed and the talk became more animated, our Swiss partners actually became excited about their prospects. And we all got pretty happy. It was a real celebration.

Of course there were changes. Kickbacks in cigarettes were quite common in Switzerland, as they were elsewhere in the world, except in the United States. We didn't do things that way, and we explained the new policy, which they had to accept.

FTR became the spearhead of our entire operation in Europe. PM's European success really started in Switzerland; what happened there opened our eyes to the entire European market, and in turn led the way for various other moves we made. The FTR purchase was one of the best we ever made. There were years, even early in the relationship, where our profits were more than half the purchase price; soon they exceeded that price.

European operations were run from a modern office building in Lausanne on the shores of Lake Geneva. I thoroughly enjoyed visiting FTR, because of the high quality of the executives there and the feeling of strength and growth they exuded. We had a chance to purchase Brinkmann's when the contract ran out. Control might have been had for $26 million. But in those days we didn't have that kind of money for such purchases, so we lost out to Rothmans. We opted for PM to go it alone. We purchased an existing building in West Berlin, where we established a factory, and initially operated out of a small suite of offices in Frankfurt.

We had almost instant success. PM expanded rapidly, purchasing an existing cigarette plant in Munich. Philip Morris GmbH has been one of the crown jewels in PM International's crown: we now have more than 40 percent of the German market.

Swiss smokers had taken to Marlboros quickly, and so did others. Italians going back and forth to Switzerland would purchase Marlboros there and bring them home. In this way, Marlboro was introduced in Italy, much to the consternation of the Italian monopoly, whose leading brand, an inexpensive cigarette called M.S., suffered as a result. In 1962 the Italian monopoly entered into an agreement with us and so we had entry into that country through a licensing agreement, and later through imports as well as from our Common Market factories. It was a tough road, but before I stepped down in 1978 we had a quarter of the Italian market.

Before the licensing arrangement, the Italian government had relied upon the tobacco monopoly as an important source of revenue. Now, as Marlboro sales cut into those of the domestic brands, the Italians had second thoughts. The monopoly tried to reduce Marlboro production in Italy, whereupon smokers turned to Marlboros coming in from Switzerland, Gibraltar, Antwerp, and North Africa. As with France, there was absolutely no chance that we could get an option on the Italian cigarette monopoly.

We kept rolling along. In 1961 we signed a licensing agreement with Hong Kong Tobacco that gave us our foothold in Asia. We followed that with further moves into Latin America. In 1966 we acquired a majority interest in a leading Argentinian manufacturer, Massalin y Celasco. By then it was clear that PM would become an important global presence.

Success brings changes and rewards. Our successes overseas caused us to rethink the corporate structure, which was changed as of January 1, 1967. We created Philip Morris Incorporated, as a holding company with three operating companies: Philip Morris Domestic, Philip Morris International, and Philip Morris Industrial. I was to be chairman and CEO of Philip Morris Inc., and Weissman was to be its president and COO. The three operating companies' presidents and COOs were to be Ross Millhiser at Domestic, Fred Stefan at Industrial, and my cousin Hugh Cullman, replacing Weissman, at International.

From the first we knew that PM International would have trouble cracking the profitable U.K. market. Not only was it

BAT's backyard, but the English had a strong preference, going back centuries, for Virginia-type cigarettes. Imperial Tobacco had two-thirds of the market, and its only real competitor, Gallaher Limited, had around a quarter of Imperial's sales, but Imperial owned 36 percent of Gallaher, so its position was impregnable. The rest of the U.K. market was taken by minor brands and a few imports. Gallaher was in poor shape, largely because it had been slow to introduce filters. Its top brand was Benson & Hedges. (As I have mentioned, PM owned that trademark in the United States and many other countries after the 1954 B&H purchase, but there were still places—the U.K. was one of them—where we did not own the trademark.)

As it happened, in 1968 Imperial decided to sell its 36 percent position in Gallaher to obtain money for something the American companies had been doing for years: diversifying. So in early 1968 Imperial made a public offering of its Gallaher shares through Morgan Grenfell and Cazenove at 20 shillings, which didn't excite too much interest at that price. Imperial was able to sell 65 percent of its Gallaher shares, and was obliged to keep the rest.

Gallaher not only would fit in well with our strategy, but we felt certain that we could energize the company and so obtain a strong position in the U.K. through their Virginia-blend cigarettes.

Hugh Cullman and I flew to London in June and told Gallaher officials there of our plan to make a tender for all the Gallaher shares. Not unexpectedly, the Gallaher management advised against accepting our offer. I went to the company's headquarters and met with the chairman. I introduced myself, and then said, "We would like to make a tender offer for your company." The chairman replied in a dry tone, "I'm sorry, but we do not intend to accept it." I walked out. The meeting took less than five minutes. That was that.

We did manage to buy Godfrey Phillips, a much smaller U.K. cigarette company with a flagship brand, Viscount, in Australia. Phillips also had footholds in New Zealand, Pakistan, and India, and it was useful to us. But the failure to take Gallaher was a disappointment.

In 1972 PM found itself in a situation somewhat like the Gallaher contest. This time it involved one of the sharpest tobacco people in the world, Anton Rupert, a South African former university professor who entered the cigarette business in 1948 by opening a small factory in his native land. It wasn't much of a company until Rupert acquired a license to sell the line of cigarettes produced by Rothmans of Pall Mall in South Africa. In 1952 Rupert produced the first king-sized filter cigarette, Rembrandt, which was a huge success in the Commonwealth market before the American filters made their splash. Two years later he purchased Rothmans.

Rupert announced that he intended to internationalize his holdings through what he called "partnership in industry," which meant he would try to acquire additional companies or enter into 50–50 partnerships where appropriate. This was a wise decision. Apartheid South Africa was an international pariah, and Rupert knew he had to move cautiously.

Flush with cash, Rupert used some of it to purchase Carreras, another British cigarette company, whose leading brand was Craven A. By the mid-1960s, Carreras had become the third-largest U.K. cigarette company, far behind BAT and Gallaher but coming up fast.

Rupert's next winner was a cigarette called Peter Stuyvesant, developed with German tobacco man Philip Reemstma. Peter Stuyvesant, whose blend was Virginia and dark tobacco, made surprising inroads in the U.K. market.

In 1972 Rupert combined his Rothmans, Rembrandt, and Carreras holdings into a new company, Rothmans International. Rothmans was a global competitor, and the American tobacco people recognized Rupert as an elemental force of nature, a man to be reckoned with.

We clashed with Rupert several times, but not in the United States, where he did not have representation. In the next chapter I'll relate how he bested us when we tried to acquire Canadian Breweries. After that tussle, Rupert acquired Brinkmann, our original German licensee. We had a strong position in Australia by then. Rupert introduced his Winfields there through his local 50-percent-owned subsidiary, Rothmans of Pall Mall (Australia), and with a copycat version of our Marlboro Man theme, hired Australian outback actor Paul Hogan to appear in his commercials. In New York we respected Rupert and looked upon Rothmans as a fine competitor—but an even more attractive potential acquisition.

Rupert was a wily character, who played the game as well as any businessman of his time. He was prepared to enter into some kind of arrangement with another company—he wouldn't indicate just what the terms might be—and knew that the way to get the best deal would be to force potential partners into a bidding war. The two most likely candidates were PM and RJR. By then we were top dog in the international field, with RJR struggling to overcome our lead. A partnership with Rothman's—or, better yet, acquisition of it—would go far to realize that ambition. In 1980 Rupert contacted Weissman and RJR CEO Paul Sticht, who had headed that company's international effort, and set things into motion.

For a while it seemed RJR had worked out an arrangement to acquire Rothmans, but then we learned that this was not the case. Rothmans was still in play, but not looking to be acquired. Rather, the company wanted a partnership with an American concern, and was very much interested in learning what we had to offer.

That was all Weissman needed to know. He contacted

Anton's son Johann Rupert, had an initial meeting in Capetown, and then went to the Rupert mansion in nearby Stellenbosch to meet with Anton. After some maneuvering and wrangling, Weissman asked him what he had in mind. The answer was short and sweet. Anton Rupert said that he would sell an indirectly held 22 percent equity and convertible bonds of Rothmans for $350 million. This wasn't a particulary attractive deal. Rupert's valuation of the interest he was selling was quite high when one considered Rothman's earnings and the size of the cigarette business. But we wanted Rothmans, so the next day we came back with an offer of $275 million, which Rupert turned down, and the deal was finalized at $350 million in May 1981. PM now would have a foothold in Rothmans, with the right of first refusal for the purchase of an additional stake.

This arrangement didn't work out as well as expected. Rothmans slowed down after the purchase, and our biggest joint venture, one in Malaysia, fizzled. Meanwhile, Marlboro's sales were growing faster than Rothmans'. It got to the point where the rationale for a takeover no longer existed, or at least wasn't as compelling as it once appeared. So in 1989 PM sold its interest to Rupert for $860 million, a better than half-billion-dollar profit on that investment. I can't say it worked out badly for PM.

In the intervening years we signed affiliate arrangements or opened for business in the Netherlands, Sweden, the Dominican Republic, Ecuador, and elsewhere. We licensed a Yugoslav company to produce Marlboros, and a Polish concern to sell them in that country. We cracked Japan, making a license arrangement with that country's monopoly to sell Marlboro and other PM brands there.

By the mid-1960s I had started serving on the boards of other companies—Ford, Bankers Trust, Levi Straus, IBM, and Braniff, among others. The kinds of people one meets on boards of major corporations are knowledgeable, smart, and aware of opportunities for PM throughout the world I should know about. Likewise, our outside directors were sources of ideas we could employ in our business. Jacques Maisonrouge, who was the head of IBM World Trade, was for a while a PM director. After one meeting he said, "Joe, if you are not in Brazil, you are not in South America."

I knew something about the Brazilian market, and our international people knew even more. Jacques was right. So we purchased Companhia de Fumos Santa Cruz in that country. Hong Kong. Egypt. Bulgaria. You name it, we were there. And not only with Marlboro. We were expanding Parliament, Philip Morris, L&M, and other brands throughout the world.

As we did we encountered anticipated marketing problems. We always thought that differences in tastes, along with tradition, would make it difficult to sell Marlboro, Parliament, and our other U.S. brands in Europe. For a while we thought advertising and promotion might give us an edge, and so they did. The Marlboro cowboy and the western theme had a certain appeal. Europeans had always been intrigued with the American West. During the nineteenth century, western novels sold well throughout Europe. Karl May, a German writer, wrote westerns his audiences gobbled up.

In our time western motion pictures drew large European audiences, and the Italians produced those "spaghetti westerns" that did so well in the 1970s. European and Asian tourists have always been drawn to the West. So the cowboy and Marlboro Country had an appeal. But Marlboro's image did not mesh with the tastes or interests of some Europeans. For them, a different approach was required.

In America, sponsorship of sporting events had become a key element for us. We tried the same in Europe, and got good results. In America the sports we sponsored were primarily football, baseball, basketball, tennis, and golf. In Europe,

Thomson had PM sponsor Formula 1 auto racing, and Marlboro logos and ads appeared in the stadiums, on jackets, cars, and other places. Aleardo Buzzi, a flamboyant Swiss national who served as head of PM Europe, was an important person in these negotiations and placements. By 1973 PM had its own racing team, which did badly at first but improved over time. What the cowboy started, the racers finished. By 1975 Marlboro had a quarter of the Italian market and had started making inroads in the tough French market as well.

The same difficulties were experienced elsewhere. The cowboy ads didn't go over too well in Argentina, where they had their gauchos. In some parts of Asia there were cultural problems to overcome, and more often than not, we succeeded. Before many other American companies learned their lessons in this regard, we made use of nationals wherever possible. Buzzi, who in time would become president of International, was a prime example of this. Andreas Gemblar, a German who was then in charge of Eastern European licensees, was another; he would become president of PM International. They had their counterparts throughout the world. But despite all this, there always were some places where we had little hope of obtaining a meaningful market share. Entering the market in China, for example, was a difficult situation.

PM International had its ups and downs during my tenure as CEO, but there were far more ups than downs. In 1972 Marlboro became the world's best-selling cigarette—three years before it became America's top seller. This is one small indication of the impact PM International had upon the firm by that time.

So George Weissman, Hugh Cullman, and John Murphy had done a terrific job. In the 1980s, PM's chairman Hamish Maxwell built upon this solid foundation, taking the company to new heights. Geoff Bible, a truly inspirational leader, has enhanced the company's position in the 1990s. Under their leadership Marlboros were advertised in all the magazines Europeans and Asians read; and airport shops and other prime locations all over the world became Marlboro country. When it came to product placement and promotion, there has been no one better in the industry.

# CHAPTER FIVE

# Diversification

*It is hard to fail, but it is worse never to have tried to succeed.*

—Theodore Roosevelt
*THE STRENUOUS LIFE*

IN THE 1960S ALL THE CIGARETTE companies diversified. There were several reasons for this, but the important factor was the attacks on us by anticigarette forces. PM and the other companies were quite prepared to defend ourselves, but we also had no idea of how the matter might be resolved. All the top tobacco executives had memories of alcohol prohibition in the 1920s. We knew that some of the wine, beer, and spirits people had been put out of business in 1921. Those who survived did so by going into other businesses.

The tobacco people had to prepare for all eventualities. So we diversified our operations. R. J. Reynolds purchased Pacific Hawaiian Products, Penick & Ford, Chun King, Patio Foods, and eventually Nabisco. American Tobacco acquired Sunshine Biscuits, Jim Beam, and many other companies. Liggett & Meyers took over at Alpo, Paddington, and Star Industries. Lorillard also bought food companies, and then was acquired by Loews. And at Philip Morris, we were part of this industry trend.

I've already discussed our acquisition of Fabriques de Tabac Réunies in 1963, an important venture that accelerated our move into the global marketplace. By then we had experience overseas, in Australia and Latin America, and so had a pretty good idea of how to go about it. That same year we purchased a company by the name of Milprint, located in Milwaukee. We thought it produced basic packaging, and since we already had done outstanding packaging work with Marlboro, we thought it was a logical enough move.

Milprint was PM's first venture outside of tobacco, the start of our diversification efforts. We paid for it with 385,000 PM shares, which worked out to around $14 million. If the Milprint owners had held on to the PM stocks they received in 1957, today the bundle would be worth approximately $7.7 *billion.*

After the purchase, we looked at Milprint and discovered that it was more of a converter than a packager. Essentially, they converted partially assembled packaging materials to finished packaging, then sent the products on to the manufacturers. Milprint had a small operation called Nicolet Paper in De Pere, Wisconsin, a few miles south of Green Bay. Its major customers were breweries, but there were others as well. Milprint wasn't a large concern, and it faced stiff competition, so profit margins were quite low.

The next year PM acquired Polymer Industries, which manufactured industrial adhesives and textile chemicals. In 1965 we folded Milprint, Nicolet, and Polymer into a new industrial products division; in time, this became Philip Morris Industrial, but it was never to be an important part of the corporation.

These were mistakes. I'd like to say they taught us a few lessons, so in retrospect it was worthwhile. Although we stumbled with other companies taken over in this period, none of them hurt us too badly, and some were quite profitable. If we had it all to do over again, we would have done it differently, probably making bigger purchases, which we didn't feel we could afford then.

As we enjoyed that great success with Marlboro and our other cigarette brands, I was developing the idea that PM shouldn't be a one-industry company. This isn't to suggest I wanted it to become a conglomerate like ITT, Textron, or LTV. Rather, the model I had in mind was American Home Products. Now, AHP wasn't a household word, but some of its companies were—Chef Boyardee, Black Flag, Primatene Mist, Preparation H, Anacin, and many more. Almost all American homes buy some AHP products, even though they don't know the parent's name.

AHP was in other fields as well, but what attracted my interest was how management there acquired so many very familiar consumer products, which churned out high-margin, terrific profits. I did not feel that Philip Morris would ever not be known as a cigarette company, especially after the introduction and success of Marlboro. But I wanted to acquire a stable of companies in the consumer products area.

Running through my mind was the idea that smokers purchase a pack or carton of Marlboro, and then keep coming back for more on a regular basis. Razor blades had the same repeat consumer pattern. This idea certainly wasn't original to me. King Gillette, who invented the safety razor a century ago and whose company became the industry's leader, knew that you could give away the razor or sell it for a low price in order to make substantial profits on blade sales. Later, Gillette expanded into ballpoint pens, with the same notion in mind.

In 1960 we purchased American Safety Razor. I knew the company very well, since at the time at the suggestion of my friend Dick Dammann, I was a member of its board. ASR had Gem and Personna blades, the former a single edge, the latter double. But it was in a weak third position behind Gillette and Schick, and soon Bic would enter the picture and make quite a splash.

Our move seemed sensible. The business was good and the profit margins satisfactory. For all of these reasons, ASR seemed a good fit for us. Besides, many of the outlets that sold cigarettes also sold razor blades. PM moved the business from Brooklyn to Staunton, Virginia, in the western part of the state, where we built a factory for ASR. Cliff Goldsmith came up with some new products for the company, and it did very well for a while.

To go with ASR, PM purchased Burma-Shave, which manufactured a well-known shaving cream. It was a rather unusual company, managed by two farm boys from Hastings, Minnesota. The purchase was handled by John Cookman, our then chief financial officer, who one day came to my office and told me the deal was set at around $1 million, so it wasn't a major step on our part.

I suppose many Americans of my generation remember those Burma-Shave signs along the highway, five or six of them in a row, maybe fifteen feet apart, with rhyming slogans which you read phrase by phrase as you zipped along at thirty-five m.p.h.:

*Within this vale*
*Of toil*
*And sin*
*Your head grows bald*
*But not your chin*
*Burma-Shave*

And this one:

*Keep well*
*To the right*
*Of the oncoming car*
*Get your close shaves*
*From the half-pound jar*
*Burma-Shave*

John Cookman told me how the two brothers handled this advertising. "Well," he said, "the Burma-Shave owners would load up their panel trucks in the morning and drive out into the countryside, and when no one was looking, they would put up their signs and then scurry away." I asked what their budget was for all of this and John replied with a straight face, "They don't have a budget."

We purchased Clark chewing gum in 1963, with the same kind of rationale we employed for ASR: gum was sold in outlets that sold cigarettes, so we thought it would be a good line extension and enable PM to capitalize on our marketing know-how. Like ASR, Clark had plenty of competition and was small in its field. Wrigley was top dog in chewing gum, Beech-Nut was strong, and there was also Dentyne. Clark's best-selling brand and most popular flavor was Teaberry. The Clark gum line was made at our Stockton Street cigarette factory in Richmond. When Cliff Goldsmith needed the space for cigarettes, Clark was sold.

In time we sold ASR to its employees after having sold Clark, in both cases for minor financial losses. By then we had a pretty good idea of why we'd failed. These minor acquisitions were perceived at PM as too small ever to mean anything to the parent company. Bright, ambitious executives thought that to be placed at Clark or ASR instead of Marlboro was to go away from the mainstream, out of the action. I didn't think this way, but such was the thinking at PM headquarters.

Then too, we didn't provide these businesses with the attention we should have. We were too busy with cigarettes. Finally, our nontobacco acquisitions were so small they had no impact on PM. In the aggregate they accounted for less than 10 percent of our revenues.

We failed in these early attempts at diversification, and it was largely my fault. We should have bought bigger companies. Later on, Hamish Maxwell led PM into one of the most successful diversification programs in American history; I as a member of the board played a very small role in what was essentially a Maxwell show. He really transformed Philip Morris by making three major acquisitions: General Foods, Kraft, and Jacobs Suchard, a large Swiss company that manufactured coffee and chocolates.

But I did manage one large and successful acquisition, which came into PM in a rather unusual fashion. In the late 1960s we became interested in acquiring Canadian Breweries, Canada's largest brewer. Canadian Breweries had a presence in the American market as well, with such fine brand names as Labatt's, Carling, Red Cap Ale, O'Keefe, and Dow Ale. The company had revenues in the mid to low $200 million area with earnings of about $15 million to $17 million.

We had gathered about $100–$150 million in cash and prepared to make a bid, only to be foiled by Anton Rupert, who already had a stake in Canadian. For a while we considered entering into a bidding war, but this made no sense. We would have pushed the price of the stock to the stratosphere, only to wind up with a minority position. So there we were, wanting to get into brewing, and losing out on Canadian Breweries to our old competitor from the international tobacco arena.

Why should a cigarette company want to acquire a

brewer? We believed marketing techniques developed for cigarettes could be transferred to beer, an idea that would influence later acquisitions. Both products are low-priced, processed from agricultural commodities, and packaged by expensive equipment; they are advertised in similar fashion. Moreover, as George Weissman put it, "Your beer drinker and your cigarette smoker are often the same guy."

One Sunday afternoon in late August 1968, I was taking a nap at home in Briarcliff Manor, when the telephone rang. It was Peter Grace, the flamboyant CEO of W. R. Grace, who I had known slightly when we attended Yale. "Joe, I'm at the Ritz Bar in Paris and it is nine o'clock at night," he said in his trademark gravelly voice.

Wondering why he would telephone me, I replied, "Good for you Peter. What are you doing there?"

"Well, I'm having a drink," he said. He continued, "Look. You guys are interested in the beer business, and you just lost your bid for Canadian Breweries."

I said, "Yes," knowing he would soon get to the point, and I already thought I knew what it was. W. R. Grace had a 53 percent interest in Miller Brewing, but had failed in its attempt to obtain the other 47 percent of the shares. They were owned by the De Rance Foundation, controlled by one Harry John, a rather eccentric character who, while quite wealthy, lived in a trailer, let his hair grow long, and wore clothes with gaping holes in them. Harry John and Peter Grace did not get along, and the word was that De Rance would sell to just about anyone but Grace. Peter Grace had been shopping his interest around, and it appeared that he was close to a deal with Don Kendall of PepsiCo. Miller would make a nice fit for PepsiCo, and Kendall had deep pockets, so I simply assumed it was a done deal.

It wasn't. On the phone Peter said, "You've got plenty of money."

I replied, "We've got some money, thank you."

"I know you do because you already had the money to put up for Canadian Breweries. Well, I want to ask you something. Would you like to buy fifty-three percent of Miller Brewing Company?"

I knew I had to be careful, because Peter Grace had bought and sold many companies. So I listened.

Peter was gracious in his own Peter Grace way. "Well, I tell you, Joe. Take your time. Let me know by noon tomorrow."

I called an emergency meeting of the PM executive committee the next morning, and told them of Peter Grace's call. George Weissman felt that Miller would make a good acquisition, and I came around to his point of view. I then met with Felix Larkin, Peter's right-hand man, and we arrived at a price for that 53 percent: $130 million, which was $10 million or so more than Kendall had offered. Peter Grace was back in New York soon after, and the deal was finalized in two days. We were in the beer business.

Every industry has its own unique features, and some attributes it shares with other industries. We didn't enter the Miller situation unaware of the nature of brewing. We had studied the beer business. And the size of the purchase was such that we didn't make it with the casualness of, say, our purchase of Burma-Shave. I've mentioned similarities of cigarettes and beer. Let me now indicate the differences, which proceeded from the industry situation at that time.

When I was younger there were many breweries in New York. I remember Rupert, whose president also ran the New York Yankees; Schaefer, Piels, Ballantine, and many others. The industry changed after World War II. National marketing developed, local breweries closed down, and the number of breweries declined steadily. For a while there were the "Big Three"—Anheuser-Busch, Schlitz, and Pabst.

This was the way it was in 1969, when between them,

they had a little more than a third of the market. That year Miller was the eighth-largest brewer, brewing 5.2 million barrels of beer, with around a 4 percent market share. To put it in other terms, in 1969, Anheuser-Busch produced 18.7 million barrels of beer for around 16 percent of the market. This put Miller ahead of such familiar brands as Heileman, Schmidt, and Schaefer.

In the 1960s Miller had become a "niche company," in that it had a beer that appealed to a particular type of person. Packaged in clear glass bottles, Miller High Life was advertised as "The Champagne of Bottled Beer," and was consumed mostly by the upscale drinker.

This was a major problem the old management hadn't sufficiently recognized. It was recognized in the industry that 20 percent of the adult population drank 80 percent of the beer. That 20 percent was composed mostly of younger blue-collar men and the advertising campaigns of the more successful beer companies were aimed at this group. There even was a name for them: "Joe Six-pack." All the companies knew this. Schaefer had a jingle that ran, "Schaefer is the one beer to have/When you're having more than one."

Wealthy people did not drink much beer, and what they did drink was often an imported variety. They drank champagne, not the champagne of bottled beer. So that image had to change.

So did the management, which committed errors that affected Miller High Life's image as a quality beer. At a time when beer drinkers were turning increasingly to canned beers, Miller remained wedded to those clear bottles. Miller's president, at the time we were looking at the company, was a former Marquette University marketing professor, Charles Miller, who was no relation to the founding Miller family. Charles Miller didn't do much to pull Miller Brewing out of its minor niche status.

Neither had his predecessor, Fred Miller. Now, Fred Miller was a scion of the founding family, and had already achieved a certain amount of fame on his own before taking on the family business: he had been part of the college football team backfield immortalized by sportswriter Grantland Rice as "The Four Horsemen of Notre Dame." The problem was, Fred's expertise seemed to have been in football, rather than beer. So we knew we were buying a niche business. Our challenge was to turn it into something bigger and better.

Later we approached Harry John and were able to acquire the De Rance Foundation's 47 percent minority interest in Miller for an additional $97 million in cash and notes, giving PM 100 percent ownership.

During our first two years of control of Miller, we gradually replaced the old management and brought in some of our seasoned veterans who had been trained in the marketing of cigarettes. But that wasn't enough: the company needed a strong new hand at the tiller. We turned to John Murphy. In 1971 he became the Miller CEO, and like the other newcomers, he had no experience in beer, but he had performed well at PM International.

Murphy wasn't overjoyed at his move to Miller, even though I considered it a promotion. He was to be given his own operation, a chance to shine. George Weissman had a similar less-than-thrilled reaction when he first went to International, and that turned out to be the key step toward his becoming my successor.

Murphy showed that he was a a quick study and that expertise in law and cigarettes indeed could be transferred to beer. It helped, to be sure, that Murphy was, as he put it, already "an Olympic-class beer drinker." One of Murphy's first moves was to drop the "champagne of bottled beer" image without relinquishing the traditional Miller drinkers. This began with the hiring of new a new ad agency, Mc-

Cann, Erickson, headed by Bill Backer. McCann's goal, as one of the account executives put it, was to "take Miller High Life out of the champagne bucket and put it into the lunch bucket without spilling a drop." In essence, Murphy was targeting the 20 percent of the population that drank 80 percent of the beer, while seeking to retain old loyalties.

As part of this strategy he changed the advertising image. Miller had been using trumpeter Al Hirt in its television commercials. Hirt was a popular figure, but he was also quite rotund, clearly the wrong image for a beer. Murphy asked McCann-Erickson to develop a new campaign. Television commercials appeared depicting workers enjoying Miller High Life at the end of the day, with the slogan "It's Miller Time." Miller soon turned to images of young adults having a good time, much as in cigarette advertisements. At first the advertisements seemed similar to those the industry had been accustomed to, but after a while differences were discerned.

Most beer advertising of the period stressed the quality of ingredients and traditional values. The slogans tended to be generalized—"Great Gusto in a Great Light Beer" for Schlitz; Rheingold's slogan, "My Beer Is Rheingold, the Dry Beer," may have been a preview of what would come from Miller, in that it was targeted at the individual drinker's identity.

"It's Miller Time," in its original phase, clearly was meant to identify High Life with its new constituency. Other advertisements would be geared to other groups. As one industry observer remarked, it was an attempt to "divide and sell." Our research indicated that print advertisements and billboards had much less impact than television. Miller advertising expenses rose, and most of its 1975 budget—98 percent—went to television.

There was more to improving Miller's image than advertising, however. Marlboro was the quality cigarette in the market. We had to do something about Miller's quality, which was below our standard. For one thing, Miller was a heavier beer than Budweiser and Coors, because the Miller brewers used too much barley and hops, which also gave it a bitter aftertaste. Miller High Life was reformulated to make it less heavy and less bitter. We also addressed quality as it related to shelf life. There is nothing worse than stale beer, and beer can start to go stale less than two weeks after bottling or canning. Miller began dating its beer, and went to a 120-day cycle, removing old beer from distributors as did Coors.

Murphy revamped the wholesaler network, eventually replacing a third of them. Where Anheuser-Busch emphasized its wholesalers, under Murphy wholesalers played a secondary role and no longer had direct access to headquarters; rather they dealt with the Miller marketing teams. Although some grumbled, the new program provided them with a great deal of advertising and promotional support, and this helped the company act quickly to shore up slippage in any particular market.

Greater stress was placed on canned beer, since market research indicated the clear bottle was not as popular as it had been. Then came the 1972 introduction of the seven-ounce "pony" bottle. There also were some new brand introductions—Miller Malt, Miller Ale, and Milwaukee Extra. None made a big impression, but they did temporarily boost volume. We put out High Life in an eight-pack of seven-ounce bottles. We reasoned that there were times when the drinker didn't want all that beer at once, and in hot weather a twelve-ounce bottle would get warm before it was finished. The people at the brewery said it couldn't be done with the machinery they had, so Murphy brought in some new equipment and did the job. This little change in the packaging turned around High Life, paying big dividends.

Breweries were failing all over the place, and Miller was

on the lookout for bargains so as to be able to increase capacity. Our most important purchase was a defunct Chicago brewer, Meister Brau, among whose brands were Meister Brau and Buckeye. Meister Brau was one of the brewers that had experimented with low-calorie beers. Its entry in this category was named "Lite" but Lite hadn't made much of an impact at the time it was acquired by Miller.

Lower-calorie beers were not new. They had been tried before and found wanting. Rheingold had Gablinger's, and its failure was generally thought to be one of the reasons for that company's decline. But the idea struck us as sound.

Low-calorie beer (slightly less than 100 calories per 12 ounces, versus 150 calories or so for regular beer) is simple enough to formulate. All the brewer has to do is raise the temperature during the brewing process, which deactivates the enzymes that produce alcohol. Then a different enzyme is activated that prevents starch from breaking down into alcohol and sugar as much as it does in standard beers. As a result, both the alcohol and sugar contents are lowered.

We ordered our brewmasters to reformulate Lite, and in two months we had what we wanted. It was more than acceptable. In fact, in 1973, in blind tests against Coors, Lite did very well. Not only was what we called "Lite Beer from Miller" good tasting, but also it cost less to brew than Miller High Life and sold at the same price, so it was therefore potentially highly profitable. Market research had indicated that, presented properly, Lite would sell well not only to weight-conscious drinkers, but also to those accustomed to drinking several cans or bottles at a time, drinkers who would consider Lite less filling.

We started to place the brand in selected local markets, and it performed well in almost all of them with a minimum of advertising. National distribution began in 1975, with the slogan, "Lite Beer from Miller. Everything You Always

Wanted in a Beer—and Less." Humorous television and print advertisements featuring former athletes were successful. In 1975 Miller sold more than 5 million barrels of Lite worth $100 million, and representing 20 percent of the company's output. Miller had grown to be the nation's fourth-largest brewer, ahead of Coors and Pabst, though still only half the size of Budweiser.

We didn't know it at the time, but in Lite we had found the beer version of Marlboro. Lite's acceptance caught even the most optimistic executives at Miller off guard; the company could not brew enough to keep up with demand. I was reminded of what happened with Marlboro after its sensational introduction. By summer, not only was Lite on allocation to wholesalers but there were spot shortages of High Life as well, as the company enjoyed a "spillover effect" unusual in the industry. Even so, the other brewing companies, unsure whether Lite was simply a flash in the pan, waited for two years before starting to bring their own versions of low-calorie beer to the market. As a result, Miller was able to solidify its foothold in this segment.

That Lite flourished as it did was an indication of an important change in attitude in a significant part of the American population, one aspect of which was a decided move against the use of alcohol. The reason was not necessarily based on morality, but rather on health consciousness in general and weight consciousness in particular.

Physical fitness was being emphasized: jogging, swimming, and marathons became popular. Diets changed: more chicken and fish, less red meat and pork. At cocktail parties and in company lunchrooms Americans compared blood pressure levels and cholesterol counts. Natural-foods shops appeared in upper-class neighborhoods and spread to urban areas across the country.

What no one else in the brewing industry seemed to realize when Miller introduced Lite was that American tastes in alcohol were at that exact time shifting toward lighter beverages. Bottled water became a status symbol; sophisticates switched from Beefeater martinis to Perrier with a twist, or a glass of chilled white wine. Light beers were to be the brewers' response to these changes. Moreover, what one writer called "the new abstinence" was not a fad, or confined to one or even several areas of consumption. The phenomenon would continue and deepen.

Given Lite's momentum, and our willingness to forgo profits for market share almost indefinitely, we thought the unthinkable—that Miller might pass Anheuser-Busch. Why not? At the time, Marlboro was growing rapidly and would soon threaten Winston as the industry's leader, an equally unthinkable situation a decade earlier. Just as Marlboro was a better cigarette in its new market segment, filters, so Lite would be the top brand in the rapidly growing reduced-calorie field.

Murphy made no secret of his ambition: to become the nation's largest brewer. "That's our goal," he told *Advertising Age* on being named "Adman of the Year" for 1977. "It has been from the day we came in. People snickered at us then, but I don't hear them now. It's not if, it's when." He hinted it would happen before the mid-1980s. In light of Miller's penetration of major markets—much of which success came at the expense of Schlitz—this didn't seem an impossible ambition. Indeed, Miller's rise in the mid-1970s was one of the most spectacular in the history of the industry.

But Anheuser-Busch was a tough competitor. For decades it fought against its two leading competitors, Pabst and Schlitz. This was more than a fight between companies: all three firms had German-American origins, so it was a family feud between companies that had been in beer for generations. Also, Anheuser-Busch was in St. Louis while Pabst and Schlitz were based in Milwaukee, so it was a battle between two Midwestern cities that had large German-American populations. Coors became a fast-growing competitor; this company, too, had a multigenerational German background. Miller was in the same tradition, but Schlitz boasted it was "The Beer That Made Milwaukee Famous." Until we came along Miller was just another second-tier beer in that city.

As I have noted, John Murphy was a cigarette man and a lawyer, not steeped in brewing, and he seemed proud of the fact. He often disparaged traditional brewers, implying that their old-fashioned methods gave him an edge in competition. This riled the old-line brewers, and none felt the sting more than August Busch. He rarely referred to Miller by name, but rather to "our friends in Milwaukee" or, disparagingly, to "the tobacco people."

In addressing wholesalers at the 1978 convention, Busch asked them not to forget that "we are at war" and that competition was good—it separated the weak from the strong. "Together we possess all the weapons necessary to compete effectively with any competitor no matter how big or how smart. We can stand the thrust of our major competitor if we rely upon and use our combined strengths and maintain our openness and complete communication." There seemed little doubt to whom Busch was referring.

The Busch-Miller contest was intense. In this period brewing, which had long been a family business, became more corporate. The major brewers grew more efficient, but some of the fun, and the mutual respect, were no longer there. Moreover, there was far more corporate hardball than had been the case earlier. For example, at distributor conferences and other trade events, Murphy charged Anheuser-Busch with deceptive advertising in claiming its beers were "natural," since tannic acid and chemically treated beechwood were used in the brewing, and carbon dioxide was mechanically injected into the beers.

Anheuser-Busch's general manager for brewing operations, Dennis Long, promptly replied that it seemed Miller was becoming paranoid about its "inability to market their product as natural." Tannin was a natural substance and in any case was settled out of the beer before it was packaged, the beechwood was not an ingredient, and the carbon dioxide was naturally injected into the beer and was produced as a result of the fermentation process.

In 1976, when Miller became the nation's fourth-largest brewery, it was busily upgrading its facility in Fulton, New York, a small town near Syracuse, and breaking ground for a new brewery in Eden, North Carolina. Miller climbed to third place the following year, when it began construction of a glass container factory near Auburn, New York, and another brewery in Irwindale, California. The following year Miller became second to Anheuser-Busch. From the time of the acquisition to 1978, we had poured some $850 million into new facilities for Miller, but profits, though improved, did not reflect this kind of investment. For several years Miller had been a drain on the company, though it turned around in 1977 and earned $76 million. But it would have to do better than that to justify so large an investment when other attractive opportunities were becoming available elsewhere.

By then, Anheuser-Busch had come up with several light beers of its own, like Natural Light, which did not do well. Lite had too much of a lead to be overtaken by a new beer, even one with an appealing name like "Natural." Busch didn't do well with Michelob Light, which had only 20 percent fewer calories than regular beer. Why they held back from formulating and then selling Budweiser Light is a mystery. Some suggested that Busch feared offending Bud drinkers by tampering with the brew. But there seemed to be no way to outsell Lite except to capitalize on "Budweiser," the industry's most powerful name. In the spring of 1981, Busch finally unveiled Bud-weiser Light in selected markets, and it soon became evident that the product was a potential big winner.

The advertising campaign was clearly aimed at Miller. The first television commercials for the beer utilized the Clydesdales. Later television spots portrayed young, robust males approaching a bartender, asking for a "Light," and, instead of a beer, getting a flashlight, blowtorch, and other items that could be classified as a light rather than a beer. Recovering, the hapless individual would amend his request to a "Bud Light," which he was then served. Anheuser-Busch hammered away at the theme for years, with good results. In 1982 Bud Light had sales of 3.9 million barrels, more than a million barrels better than Natural Light, and three years later sales came to 5.5 million barrels. By then, however, Lite was selling 18.7 million barrels, holding and even expanding its lead.

Lite Beer from Miller was going great but when Bud Light and, later, Coors Light came out, the clutter of light beers in the market confused beer drinkers who had just been asking for a "light" beer. "Light" could mean Bud Light, Coors Light, or Miller Lite. To solve this confusion and establish the name "Miller Lite," I had to go to great lengths to get Miller to change the packaging so that the brand became "Miller Lite" and not just any "light." I'm happy to report that now people ask for a *Miller* Lite and the Miller Lite brand is doing much better. It took me many years to convince John Murphy and his successors, but I am really pleased and I feel that I made a contribution to Miller sales by insisting on a name and packaging change.

This is not to say that Miller was enjoying continued un-alloyed good fortune. High Life sales dropped and the beer's market share declined. There were several reasons for this. The "Miller Time" campaign had become outworn. "We stuck to it until it was wallpaper," Murphy conceded. By 1983 one of the jokes going around the industry was embodied in a mock slogan: "It's Miller time. Give me a Bud."

For its flagship brand, Anheuser-Busch inaugurated a new slogan: "For all you do, this Bud's for you," this being a clear response to the personal approach of "Miller Time." This new approach was quite effective for Budweiser. In the end Miller didn't become the leading brewer. But the number two position wasn't all that bad. This was one acquisition that worked out pretty well.

I can't say the same for our attempt to crack into the soft-drink business. In 1978 I had some conversations with PepsiCo regarding a possible merger. Gus Levy of Goldman Sachs, the "Mr. Wall Street" of his time, and I thought it made abundant good sense. At the time PepsiCo was in second place in soft drinks, and PM was behind RJR in cigarettes. Both companies were in consumer products, and each was known for its marketing skills. PepsiCo had Frito-Lay, the leading manufacturer of snacks, and we had Miller. The discussions went on for quite a while, and on several occasions the merger came close to realization. But ultimately nothing came of it, perhaps because each side wanted to control the merged operation.

I continued to believe PM had a future in soft drinks, and that soft drinks were a logical extension of our businesses. Coca-Cola and PepsiCo were leaders in the cola segment of the soft-drink market, which was almost two-thirds of the total. But while they had entries in other soft drinks, in the citrus area they were far behind 7-Up. The industry's third-largest company, with about 7 percent of the market and sales of $250 million, 7-Up was far and away the leader in citrus, with its lemon-lime-flavored soda.

The 7-Up people had advertised their drink as the "Uncola," referring to the fact that it was the nation's leading noncola soft drink, and it was free of caffeine, which at that time was in second place to nicotine and tar among those people who asserted the public was being inundated with cancer-causing substances. There was some talk that caffeine caused breast and pancreatic cancer, that it accelerated the heartbeat and constricted blood vessels. The cola companies were about to bring out caffeine-free versions to meet this objection, but 7-Up was there already, advertising that it had never had caffeine, and never would.

I learned that 7-Up's management had been considering selling the company, and would give us an interested hearing. The company was receiving good publicity, sales and earnings were high, and management wanted to get out at the top. For our part, we thought the top wasn't there yet. So we began negotiations, although it seemed clear from the start 7-Up wanted an all-cash offer and we were prepared only for a stock swap.

This difference in financing was only one problem I faced on this deal. The other, more serious one was a disagreement I had with PM senior management, many of whom did not want 7-Up. Ross Millhiser, who by then was PM's president, was for tobacco pure and simple. We had a winner in cigarettes, and ventures away from cigarettes would hurt profit margins, earnings, and growth. Besides, we knew nothing about soft drinks, and earlier purchases, except for Miller, hadn't turned out well. Finally, there were Coke and Pepsi, who could make an important assault against 7-Up if they chose to do so, which they would if and when PM managed to increase its market share substantially. It was easy to imagine Coke putting on a major campaign for Sprite, its lemon-lime soft drink, which was a 7-Up look-alike, and cutting sharply into 7-Up's customer base. This was what happened when Miller started moving up against Anheuser-Busch, and there was no reason to expect soft drinks to be different.

Millhiser had a strong ally in Cliff Goldsmith, then the head of Philip Morris USA (previously Philip Morris Domestic), who was another tobacco man. He conceded that Miller was successful, but noted that it had taken an enormous amount of badly needed capital to achieve its market position and was taking additional capital away from cigarettes, where profit margins were much better. All this seemed to indicate that if Miller, and by extension 7-Up, did badly, we would suffer, while on the other hand success would also bring problems.

The purchase of 7-Up was also opposed by PM's chief financial officer, Shepard Pollack, who knew the numbers well, and by our brilliant marketing guru, Jack Landry. The bottom line for Landry, Pollack, Goldsmith, and Millhiser was the same: stick to what you know, cigarettes.

The objections of Goldsmith and Millhiser might be understood in the light of their loyalty to cigarettes, but Jetson Lincoln, who was our leading corporate planner and as such had investigated 7-Up carefully, pointed out to us that the industry itself presented problems, and that 7-Up's were more serious than Coke's and Pepsi's. In the soft-drink industry the large companies formulated the syrups, and independent bottlers purchased the syrup and ran their territories as they saw fit. These bottlers had more power than did the distributors in beer. The distributors had to purchase the beer from the brewery and shipment could be canceled if their efforts were unsatisfactory. Beer distributor investments were small, limited to warehouses, trucks, and the like. The bottlers had large investments in factories and machinery as well, and had responsibility for local advertising and promotion.

The large bottlers handled several brands of soft drinks from different companies. So a 7-Up bottler often also had a tie-in with Coke or Pepsi. This meant that even if we wanted to come out with a competitor for Coke and Pepsi in the cola area, we would face opposition from our bottlers, who then might give up on us and start selling the cola company's lemon-lime drinks.

I did have some support among top management. George Weissman, who was by then vice chairman, brought up the ever-present health issue. Everything Millhiser and Goldsmith said might be true, he argued, but what about that continuing assault against smoking? We thought our position was strong, and that we could throw back our critics in the courts and in the legislatures. But what if we were wrong? What if sometime in the future our cigarette business was hurt by taxes, legislation, a turn in public opinion, or even outright attempts at prohibition? We would have a very nice beer business and perhaps a few very small odds and ends—along with lawsuits well into the next century. Weissman was of the opinion that we had to expand into new areas, and soft drinks were a natural outlet for our talents. Like Miller, 7-Up could use our marketing and advertising expertise. Like beer and cigarettes, soft drinks were a low-priced, easily accessible product. Moreover, Weissman, who had worked so well with Murphy, told us that in Murphy we had a man who understood the beverage business. What he had done with Miller, said Weissman, he could do with 7-Up. I like to think I decided the matter on its merits. In the end PM purchased 7-Up for $514 million.

To run 7-Up we selected Ed Frantel, Murphy's vice president for sales at Miller, who immediately set out on four missions somewhat reminiscent of Murphy's successful efforts at Miller. Frantel increased advertising coverage, concentrating on the caffeine matter. He also reformulated the syrup, substituting fructose for sucrose. This cut costs somewhat, but that wasn't the reason for the change. Rather, Frantel was seeking a better, longer-lasting taste. He ran into problems here, because the bottlers did not do their jobs correctly, and the result was a soft drink inconsistent in color and flavor, which hurt us for a while.

At the same time he started purchasing bottlers, both to give him more control over the product and to prepare the way for the fourth step. In 1982 7-Up launched its own cola drink, Like. The name clearly alluded to Lite, which had turned things around for Miller. "You don't need caffeine. And neither does your cola," was the ad pitch. But this didn't work out as well as we thought it would.

Going up against Coca-Cola and PepsiCo with a different soft drink was not the same as competing with Anheuser-Busch with a light beer. Coke and Pepsi had more clout with the independent bottlers than we did; they had shelf space in the supermarkets, and influence with other customers. When we took over at 7-Up, the soft drink was sold in 17,000 McDonald's. Coke went to McDonald's, talked them into replacing 7-Up with Sprite, and that was the end of our beverage relationship with McDonald's.

We made some fundamental mistakes. We told the distributors that we would pay for national advertising, and they could then spend their money on promoting 7-Up with more displays and the like. Well, the distributors decided that since we were picking up the tab for 7-Up advertising, they could use the money to promote their other brands: Dr. Pepper, Royal Crown, and so on.

Then too, perhaps we moved too fast. In retrospect it is easy to say that if we had first consolidated 7-Up's market position and then moved into Like, we would have succeeded. Then again, perhaps we would have failed anyway. Though 7-Up was making progress, it was not as fast as we would have liked, and the company was eating up cash. Millhiser and Goldsmith didn't say too much about this, but the 7-Up people, Weissman, and I knew that the old comradeship that had existed prior to the acquisition had been strained. By 1984 our two largest acquisitions were performing unsatisfactorily. Miller was profitable, but its early rapid growth had slowed, and the company was burdened by excess capacity from that breakneck construction program. And 7-Up was in the red.

Long before that, in 1978, I had stepped down as PM's chairman and CEO. I was still active in corporate matters, and had become chairman of the executive committee. Weissman became PM's chairman and CEO, Millhiser vice chairman, and Goldsmith president, while Hugh Cullman headed PM USA. Murphy was given responsibility for 7-Up and Mission Viejo as well as Miller. Hamish Maxwell moved into the presidency of PM International.

A few words about Mission Viejo, which has since been sold. This was a real estate venture that had nothing to do with our other businesses and never accounted for more than a few percentage points in our overall sales. Chandler Kibbee, the former CFO of Philip Morris, led us into this area because of the 1970s boom in real estate. He was concerned that we would have an excessive cash flow. Mission Viejo has approximately 100,000 acres of land in southern California and south of Denver, Colorado, and was engaged in developing parcels for community development and home building.

The centerpiece was a 10,000-acre parcel in Orange County near Laguna Beach, where we constructed a town called, appropriately enough, Mission Viejo. By 1980, when the real estate boom started to fizzle, it had a population of 44,000, living in 13,000 homes. The community had golf courses, tennis courts, shopping centers, and schools, everything a town is supposed to have. That year Mission Viejo accounted for 8 percent of all the homes sold in Orange County, so it was a major force. Its fate was tied into the economy of the area. When California's growth slowed down in the 1980s, so did our little real estate operation. When it started to pick up in the 1990s, so did Mission Viejo. We held on to it for a while longer, but didn't go any further in real estate.

Mission Viejo was an opportunistic investment, taken in the spirit of the venture capitalists of the time. Philip Morris had no intention of becoming a major force in real estate, but instead hoped to capitalize on a fine opportunity, which indeed the land venture was. In 1996 the Mission Viejo company had revenues of $157 million. This was a flyspeck in the PM picture, but the real estate market in that part of the country had revived enough that we used Morgan Stanley to find a buyer. The median price of single-family homes in the area rose 4.3 percent in June 1997, the largest increase since 1991. PM sold the Mission Viejo company to the J. F. Shea construction company at a big profit and so exited the real estate business. No one really noticed except for those involved.

In 1986 PM had sold 7-Up. There were two reasons for this. In the first place, by then it had become apparent that this was another Joe Cullman plan that didn't work out well. I'll admit that 7-Up was a mistake. I know that some would say it is another demonstration of the wisdom of sticking to your core business and not diversifying into related areas. This is the conventional wisdom of 1998. But it wasn't the gospel at the time we started diversifying in the 1960s. Then the pundits talked about spreading the risk, balancing products and services under the corporate umbrella, building on demonstrated corporate talents, and a lot more. So we went with the flow in the 1970s, and I have no apologies to make on that score.

I don't think too highly of executives who are too cautious. Had Murphy been cautious at Miller he would have concentrated on High Life and not gone into Lite Beer. At

PM we would have concentrated on Philip Morris and not backed Marlboro, Merit, Benson & Hedges, and Virginia Slims. For that matter, we wouldn't have gone into the international sphere the way we did.

One lesson I did learn was that a company the size of Philip Morris had to go into new areas in a big way. Mission Viejo meant so little to us that no one at Philip Morris who had talent and ambition wanted to go there. I have described how Murphy was concerned about his switch to Miller, and how Weissman had to be assured that his transfer to overseas was an opportunity. Another reason for large acquisitions is that if you intend to diversify, you have to do it in a meaningful fashion. Mission Viejo was small.

Hamish Maxwell understood this, and did something about it: he sold 7-Up. Maxwell proved his skill at takeovers, bringing three major companies into the Philip Morris fold and changing its direction considerably. In late 1984 there were many discussions regarding who would succeed Weissman. John Murphy had a shot at the top job, but some felt he had most recently been associated with the nontobacco end of the business, and his selection would send out the wrong signals.

By 1984 both Miller and 7-Up were in the doldrums, and that hurt Murphy's chances. Instead, the board turned to Maxwell, a jovial, intelligent, experienced Scotsman who had arrived at PM in 1954, the same year I did, and rose up through the ranks in tobacco. His father, Sandy Maxwell, had been head of the British Tobacco Council, organized to represent the tobacco industry in its relationships with the British government and in other external relations. Hamish started out as a salesman at PM USA and went on from there to more senior positions. Then he moved to PM International and headed our Asia-Pacific operations. This provided him with some very good experience, because although we are now the leading manufacturer in Australia, we had a tough time at the beginning.

In the eighties, as chairman and CEO, Maxwell had two choices. The cigarette business was throwing off tremendous profits. Given that we had to sell 7-Up, and that the slowdown at Miller meant it would not need the kind of capital it had gobbled in the 1980s, he could either pay out large dividends and enter into a massive stock buyback program, or make acquisitions. Corporations are like sharks. Unless they keep moving ahead, they go down. Maxwell opted to keep moving.

I will not go into Maxwell's acquisitions in too much detail, because they are his story, not mine. As for me, when I stepped down from an active role at the company I maintained my office at 100 Park Avenue, where quite a few of PM's retired top executives have tenth-floor offices. (In 1983, PM built its own twenty-six-story headquarters building across Forty-first Street at 120 Park Avenue.) I was available for consultation, to attend meetings, and for anything else the company needed. In time Weissman, Murphy, Millhiser, and Maxwell would arrive. The ranks of offices at 100 Park reminded one visitor of the miles and miles of old warplanes out in the open at an airfield near Tucson, Arizona. He said that you could stroll down the aisle and see more than half a century of PM history. Others have called the occupants of the tenth-floor executive offices "the wizards of was."

Back to Hamish Maxwell and acquisitions. In the first place, he wanted healthy companies. There would be no more turnarounds obtainable at bargain prices. Nor did Maxwell want to purchase smaller companies in the hope of growing them over a long period. In other words, no more Milprints, 7-Ups, Clarks, American Safety Razors, or Mission Viejos. Maxwell wanted companies that could benefit from PM's expertise in marketing, meaning they should be in packaged consumer goods with well-known brand names. All signs pointed to branded foodstuffs, the kind sold in supermarkets.

But such companies presented some troubles. Their profit margins were far below those of cigarettes. On the other hand, their price/earnings multiples were higher than those of the stocks of tobacco companies due to the health issue.

Financing such large acquisitions was akin to arranging for the docking of a supercarrier. One slip could lead to major problems. Maxwell figured he would have to pay cash for such acquisitions, because a stock tender would dilute PM seriously. He would put up cash from our fairly substantial treasury and the sale of 7-Up, and then borrow the rest short term.

At the time—the mid-1980s—interest rates were falling and appeared likely to continue to do so, which would be helpful. The acquired company's earnings should more than cover the interest on the debt. This was important, because large food companies tended to have steady if not exciting earnings. We could pay off the principal with cigarette earnings and, we hoped, with the additional earnings from the acquired company once we got going there. So that was the basic game plan. The next step was to select a target.

It wasn't all too difficult. There are just so many major companies that filled our requirements. They included such familiar names as General Foods, Carnation, Nabisco, Pillsbury, Kraft, Campbell, Heinz, Borden, Quaker Oats, Ralston Purina, General Mills, and Beatrice. We weren't the only one eyeing these companies. Nestlé got Carnation; R. J. Reynolds purchased Nabisco and became RJR Nabisco; Britain's Grand Metropolitan purchased Pillsbury; and, after several different owners, ConAgra acquired Beatrice.

General Foods was the biggest of them all, with $9 billion in sales, nearly half PM's revenues. The company's brands were familiar to all Americans—Maxwell House

Coffee, Post cereals, Oscar Mayer meats, Jell-O, and many more.

At first glance General Foods seemed like an elephant compared to PM's greyhound. General Foods was big and powerful, but relatively slow-moving, while PM was innovative, swift, and ever alert. Much of this had to do with the nature of the business. All the food companies innovate, and all the big ones are keen on marketing, but there isn't much one can do to alter the content or image of Jell-O or Grape-Nuts.

GF had been pretty good at acquiring companies to round out its line—aggressive companies that, once they achieved a niche, were no longer as aggressive as they once were. These included Entenmann's, Oscar Mayer, and Louis Rich. General Foods appeared to be sluggish, and was perceived by some as having management problems.

The decision to make a play for General Foods was approved by the board. GF didn't approach us; we approached them. Bruce Wasserstein of the financial consulting firm Wasserstein & Perella was the person who advised us, and he did it very well.

Maxwell knew the tender offer we were preparing would be ill-received by management of the target company. This was the age of the hostile takeover, complete with poison pills, shark repellents, and golden handshakes. Maxwell lined up his bankers in advance, and then shocked the financial community with a $120 per share offer, all cash, for a stock that had been selling for around $80. It was a substantial premium, one that would frighten away other potential suitors, and a price General Foods' management could hardly say understated the company's value. So getting GF was no problem. Turning it into a more profitable company was the real challenge.

It began quickly. Out went some old managers and in came new ones, mainly from junior positions at GF. We cut the payroll and initiated a program to reinvigorate the coffee business, which took some doing. I remember the time, early in the PM–General Foods relationship, when the PM board learned there were large amounts of substandard coffee on store shelves. Someone at the meeting asked what would happen to that coffee, and the GF answer was that it would flow through to the consumer. This was completely alien to the PM approach. Over a period of time we had to convince the GF people that they had to be completely wedded to the concept of top quality, always. This came across in time, and GF was turned around, although as a result of the takeover, profit margins for PM on the whole fell.

The GF experience taught us a few things. First of all, you have to know what you are talking about and be damn sure you are right in so large an undertaking, because if you aren't, disaster awaits. Then you have to talk to the target's management about problems and issues and level with them. We always worked that way. I started our Corporate Products Committee years ago. It meets ten Mondays a year, before the board meeting, and settles issues relating to quality, product changes, and packaging. I would also suggest that the acquiring company make certain the acquired company understands the corporate culture they are going to encounter. We have our standards in products and people, and companies that PM acquires have to understand this thoroughly.

Additionally, the leadership at the company to be acquired must appreciate that they are going to have to accept changes; otherwise, they should remain independent or find some other suitor with whom they would be more compatible. The major problem comes when the acquired company is family run or headed by a founder. Leadership at such firms often has a tough time adjusting to new concepts.

Maxwell used a twofold strategy to complete his acquisition program. One planned aspect was the purchase of another large company, preferably one that didn't need the stimulation that GF required. The other part of the plan was to obtain a set of top managers to direct the entire food operation. And that brought us to Kraft. Kraft was to cheese what General Foods was to coffee. Kraft was a $10 billion company, which in addition to Kraft cheeses, had such products as Miracle Whip, Parkay, Tombstone Pizza, Velveeta, and Philadelphia Brand Cream Cheese.

The fit with GF was good. But Kraft CEO John Richman didn't want to be taken over. This presented a problem, but not an insurmountable one. Maxwell contacted Richman, told him PM was prepared to pay $90 a share for Kraft, which would make it a $11.5 billion deal, and gave him some time to think it over. There was some parrying; the amount offered went up and down. PM's final offer was $13.1 billion and the deal was finalized. Thus was created Kraft General Foods. Now PM was not only the world's largest cigarette company, it was also the largest food company in North America and the second-largest food company in the world. It still is.

Maxwell then began seeking acquisitions that could enhance our food business. To reiterate, he wanted big companies, for once an enterprise gets to be as large as PM, only major acquisitions will have an impact on operations. One such company was Jacobs Suchard A.G., a coffee, chocolate, and candy giant which was controlled by Klaus Jacobs, a Swiss businessman.

Jacobs Suchard had Swiss firms Suchard and Tobler, two of the premium quality names in chocolate, and Côte d'Or, a quality Belgian company, as well as Italy's Du Lac and Greece's Palvides. The Jacobs part of the business was the largest coffee operation in Europe. Exposure to the American market was limited to E. J. Brach, which made various candies including jelly beans.

Jacobs was interested in expansion in the American market. He knew of the troubles General Foods was having with coffee, and in 1990 approached Maxwell about a possible purchase of the General Foods coffee business. When Maxwell did not appear interested, Jacobs came back with another idea. Would PM be interested in purchasing Jacobs Suchard? Jacobs' price was reasonable—$3.7 billion—without Brach, an operation PM did not want anyway. So Maxwell took it to the board, and we had to consider it seriously.

Jacobs Suchard was certainly large, with $4.7 billion in revenues. It was not as profitable as our other food holdings, but this was the case with many European food companies, most of which were limited to the small national markets. This question of scale could be a problem. W. R. Grace had attempted to gobble mid-sized national companies to create a "General Foods of Europe," and then take the national companies international. The attempt failed, and Grace eventually sold off these holdings.

But the situation was changing. The European Economic Community was going to become a reality in 1992, and perhaps internationalization would then be possible. Besides, our Kraft General Foods operations in Europe were limited, and a merger with Jacobs Suchard would instantly transform us into a major player on that continent.

So we purchased Jacobs Suchard. Once more, that terrific cash flow from cigarettes financed a major purchase outside the tobacco area. PM now had a strong global cigarette company, and a strong international food operation.

# CHAPTER SIX

# *Conservation*

*The nation behaves well if it treats the natural resources as assets which it must turn over to the next generation increased, and not impaired in value.*

*Conservation means development as much as it does protection.*

—Theodore Roosevelt
THE NEW NATIONALISM

I SUPPOSE MY LOVE OF WILDLIFE goes back to my earliest days, when my dad took me to Belgrade Lakes in Maine to go fishing. I must have been six years old the first time we went there, and I've loved fishing ever since.

I've loved being in wild environments for as long as I can remember. My first wife's family had a wonderful place in the Adirondacks called the Kildare Club. It has some of the best trout fishing I know of, and I still go there.

In 1896 the Lehman family acquired the Kildare property northwest of Tupper Lake, New York, in the Adirondack Mountains. It was sold by the Vanderbilt Webb family, the builders of the Adirondack division of the New York Central Railroad. The Adirondack division ran from the town of Schenectady, New York, to Lake Placid and connected with the New York and Ottawa Railroad, which ran from Tupper Lake to Ottawa, the capital of Canada.

The new owners of Kildare had their own railroad station on the Tupper Lake–Ottawa line. They'd take the train from Grand Central Terminal in New York City, a sleeper, get off at Tupper at five A.M., and take the Ottawa train north to Kildare about seven A.M. Then they went by vehicle up a bumpy dirt road to the magnificent clubhouse on Jordan Lake.

The 10,000-acre property had two other bodies of water, Amber Lake to the north and Otter Pond to the east. The Jordan River, a narrow but productive native brook trout river, crossed the property and provided outstanding fishing, producing trout of up to three pounds, one of which I caught with Marian Sulzberger Heiskell. The virgin, never logged woods of coniferous and deciduous stands were full of game and birds, especially white-tailed deer, black bear, and red fox, plus ruffed grouse and the rare spruce grouse. Kildare was typical of the other great camps of the Adirondacks so popular at the turn of the century and later, as for example the fabled Whitney Park of 55,000 acres to the south.

I first visited Kildare with Sue in the spring of 1935. We were engaged and were to be married that summer. It was truly a breathtaking experience—fourteen miles from anyplace by private road, short on limited modern conveniences but long on wildlife and privacy. It was an experience that would affect my entire life and those of my family and friends.

Today, a hundred years after it was purchased, it is still a pristine return to nature for me, my daughter, Dorothy Treisman; her sons, Joel and Jeffrey, and other family and old friends. I still fish for the native brook trout and hunt the elusive whitetail, although the camp has been made more comfortable. It's still a place to go to clear my mind of all the clutter of our world and to commune with nature. It's in the Adirondack Park which, thanks to Governor Nelson Rockefeller, consists of 6 million acres of protected wilderness beauty.

Years ago the first Philip Morris five-year-plan meeting was held at the Kildare Club. When I got a two-week leave from the Navy in 1944 after two years in the Pacific, I spent a week of it at Kildare. On the cruiser *Montpelier* in the Pacific, I daydreamed about the air, the trees, the lake, and the trout fishing at Kildare.

Sue gave me her share in Runnymede, a marvelous place in Atlantic Canada, on the Restigouche River. There I have fished for Atlantic salmon since 1947. Runnymede has provided me with some of the happiest moments of my life. Nearby, I also share the Two Brooks camp on the Upsalquitch River, a tributary of the Restigouche, with my brother Edgar and before that with Ted Bensinger of the Brunswick Corporation. We first leased Two Brooks water in 1962 from the Province of New Brunswick and bought the camp for $10,000.

Atlantic salmon fishing is an all-absorbing sport. When you're casting for salmon from a canoe or wading, your mind is occupied so completely, your problems and the world's problems vanish in the clean, beautiful air.

The biggest Atlantic salmon I ever landed had an estimated weight of forty-seven pounds. After measuring its length and girth, we released it. It was taken at the home pool at the famous BrandyBrook Camp on the Restigouche River in Atlantic Canada. It was 1969, late in the season in August of a bad year. We had seen this monster lying in low water at a cold brook inlet into the Restigouche. Lorne Irvine, the caretaker at Runnymede, and I had already fished over him. At dark we were returning to the dock when Lorne said, "Give him one more try." I said, "You try." He did and failed.

I tried something different. I threw a size 8 Green Highlander three feet beyond the nose of the salmon and hauled it toward me. The water erupted as the great fish struck the fly with a vengeance. He came way out of the water—glistening in the dusk. I set the hook and was fast to the biggest salmon I've ever seen. My nine-foot, three-inch Hardy rod bent double. The Bogden reel screamed but the huge fish stayed hooked. Then the backing on the reel jammed and we had to follow the huge fish around the pool. One and a half hours later we brought him alongside our canoe. I was exhausted and so was the fish, but he swam away when released. Our Atlantic Salmon Federation studies show that 90 percent of all salmon released survive.

Through my love for salmon fishing I became involved in the work of this group, the world's leading Atlantic salmon conservation organization. For many years the only organization in the world of any consequence that addressed the problem of salmon overharvesting was the Canadian-based Atlantic Salmon Association, formed in 1948. The reason there was no earlier organized group was that until the mid-twentieth century Atlantic salmon were plentiful. In fact, lumbermen used to stipulate in their contracts that they did not have to eat salmon more than five days a week. Salmon were used for fertilizer in those days.

In 1968 scientists discovered the winter feeding grounds of the Western Hemisphere Atlantic salmon, in the Davis Strait off Greenland. Atlantic salmon were being excessively netted there. Salmon buffs tried to get the Danes, who owned Greenland, to intervene, but to no avail. Finally, the U.S. Congress passed the historic Pelley Act in the 1970s which permitted a boycott of products from any country that did not practice conservation.

For some time Atlantic salmon fishermen who lived in the United States but fished in Canada had been unhappy about the relative lack of effective conservation results by the Atlantic Salmon Association. Many U.S.–based Atlantic salmon buffs with properties in Atlantic Canada were concerned by the drop in the Atlantic salmon population, and they decided to do something about it. In 1968, in order to address the Atlantic salmon problems, several of us decided to form an American equivalent of the Canadian organization. The new group was called the International Atlantic Salmon Foundation (IASF).

The IASF was formed one evening in the spring of 1969 in Dudley Mills's small apartment in New York. To launch IASF a significant amount of money was raised, about $400,000, from a small group including Seward Johnson, Charles Englehard, and Frank Goelet. Seward Johnson led off the gifts by donating $250,000. B. E. "Ted" Bensinger was also present, and played a key role soon after in finding Dr. Wilfred Carter.

Wilfred Carter was a ten strike. He was the soul and character of the IASF and then the ASF, since we merged the Canadian and U.S. organizations to form the Atlantic Salmon Federation. He served for years as president and is now president emeritus of ASF. He has been a vital source of strength in Atlantic salmon conservation for thirty years.

I first heard about him 1969, when Ted Bensinger telephoned me to tell me about this Canadian aquatic biologist whom he wanted to hire at $10,000 a year to head the organization. Carter took office on October 1, 1969. He lived at Gaspé, Quebec, and our first "headquarters" was a converted guesthouse in the rear of his property, with two desks and chairs, one filing cabinet, one typewriter, and one telephone. The budget for that first year was $93,589. It's now more than $4 million. Carter was the first employee, and he led the movement to restrict salmon fishing and the fight to restore the salmon population to acceptable levels.

The beginnings were modest, but the results were significant. The Atlantic Salmon Association had warned of dire consequences if the Atlantic salmon kill was not carefully regulated. This led, as I said, to the formation in the United States of the International Atlantic Salmon Foundation, which in addition to its other work, became an effective lobbying group.

The first and perhaps most important crisis we faced involved that Greenland overharvesting problem. The Atlantic salmon does swim upstream and spawns, but doesn't die as the Pacific salmon does. Instead, it returns to the Atlantic. One Atlantic salmon can repeat this cycle six or more times in a lifetime. Many salmon spawn in eastern Canadian rivers and then return to the sea and the Greenland area, where they meet drift-netting vessels from several countries; the next year far fewer of them return to Canada. We calculated that as many as 600,000 salmon a year were being harvested by the Greenlanders. To address this problem, the Committee on the Atlantic Salmon Emergency (CASE) was organized by the IASF, and this led the way in 1972 to an agreement with the Greenlanders to restrict offshore drift netting and establish quotas for takes.

Getting rid of those nets and others meant that many salmon could return to spawn in the rivers where they were born, without being netted in wholesale quantities. This was a huge step. We convinced the public that the Atlantic salmon is worth saving, and it is. The Federation also engages in widespread education in Atlantic salmon conservation. For years the Canadian government has restricted fishing for Atlantic salmon to fly fishing only throughout Canada.

What about the commercial fishermen? Didn't our actions cause them hardship? The answer is mixed. Had commercial fishing continued at the rate it was going, the fishermen would have put themselves out of business due to a lack of salmon. We held generally amicable discussions with reliable commercial fishermen who supported a salmon conservation program. When we began there were some 3,000 netters. The Canadian federal government bought out all but a hundred. They understand that our efforts in this area will help result in the survival of the Atlantic salmon species.

Of equal concern to us were the Native Canadians, who had fished for salmon for thousands of years, but had in recent years adopted modern technology and increased their netting activities once the commercial netters were bought out. We have tried to get them to cut back, but with limited success.

Another idea, aquaculture, was developed successfully. Most of the world's table-consumed salmon are now "ranch" raised, and this helps preserve the wild salmon in the oceans and rivers. These salmon ranches are very successful and have helped reduce the pressure on wild Atlantic salmon. Before we started out with aquaculture, the table demand for salmon was far greater than supply, and so prices rose sharply. When ranch-raised fish came to market, prices fell, so that by 1997 the price was often only five cents a pound and the ranch fishing interests were battling to raise prices, with the ranchers competing with the remaining commercial netters. The fight to save the Atlantic salmon is not over by a long shot.

The ASF didn't stay small for long, and its influence expanded exponentially. I devoted a good deal of my time to this project, especially after I retired as Philip Morris CEO in 1978. Because of the Atlantic Salmon Federation, at first with Wilf Carter and later with Bill Taylor in leadership positions, and because of their work and that of others in the organization, we hope future generations of salmon fishermen will be able to enjoy the sport.

Many readers may not share my passion for angling for Atlantic salmon. In fact, to them it may seem hard to understand. All I ask is for these people to imagine being in a canoe or wading on a salmon river when all is still and you are alone or with a close friend, with the sun setting and the smell of pine trees in the air. You are casting for salmon, and after a while you hook one. The rod bends sharply, a struggle ensues, and in the end, if you are skilled enough or lucky enough, you net the fish, and if it is legal to keep, a little while later it is grilling over an open fire. You are about to have a meal to rival any found in the world's best restaurants, in a beautiful, sylvan setting. Life doesn't offer much better than this.

My interest in the outdoors led me to several other important conservation efforts. When I was in school, Teddy Roosevelt became a great hero of mine, in part because of his great dedication to conservation. He led us to understand that conservation means preserving our natural wildlife and habitat for later generations. This means maintaining and improving the purity of water in the lakes and rivers, safeguarding the forests and grasslands, and protecting the wildlife that lives there. It means maintaining the planet as we inherited it. People have to be educated about the importance of their environment.

There are so many individuals and organizations today involved in conservation and preservation and this has led to a greater appreciation of nature and the environment. The World Wildlife Fund, to which I devote considerable time and effort, is the best-known group in the world. Its enlightened leadership today includes President Kathryn Fuller and Chairman Roger Sant. It distributes more than $75 million annually on worthwhile projects worldwide. The World

With Billie Jean King, Chris Evert, Rosie Casals, and Virginia Wade, celebrating the Virginia Slims Championship.

Members of the International Tennis Hall of Fame in 1994. *Front row, left to right:* Stan Smith, Hana Mandlikova, Bud Collins, and Gardnar Mulloy. *Back row:* Angela Mortimer Barrett, Sidney Wood, Fred Perry, Frank Parker, myself, Don Budge, Pauline Betz Addie, Tony Trabert, William Talbert, Dennis Ralston, and Vic Seixas.

On my head, 1987.

With William McChesney Martin, former chairman of the Federal Reserve Board and cofounder of the Tennis Hall of Fame.

With my friend Arthur Ashe.

This is the official picture for my induction into the Tennis Hall of Fame.

Joan and I enjoy the Virginia Slims Tennis Tour.

Mr. and Mrs. Joseph F. Cullman 3rd at our second wedding, in 1988.

With Joan at a recent function in New York City.

Still great friends after more than fifty years—Johnny Wolf and I at Martha's Vineyard, 1985.

In Kenya, 1967, with Bob Marschalk and his one-hundred-pound elephant tusks.

At the Serengeti in 1997. Terry Mathews, Derek Hurt, myself, Tracy Straus, and Lucy Danziger. Our driver and Kay Delaney Bring are on the roof.

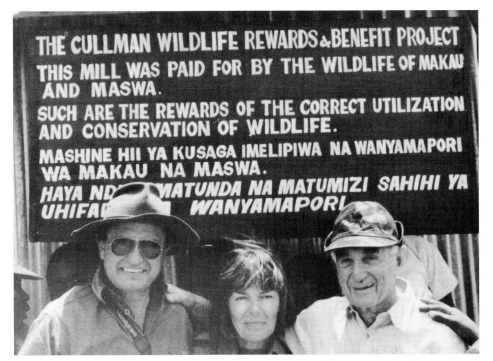

Robin Hurt poses with Joan and me at a Cullman Wildlife Project south
of the Serengeti.

Kathryn Fuller and Russell Train honor me as the first and only honorary trustee
of the World Wildlife Fund.

A great trout! This picture was taken by my aide Frank Gryboski.

Chris Evert and her husband Andy Mill with me on the Restigouche.

The great outdoorsman and my good friend Lee Wulff upon my election as president of the Atlantic Salmon Federation.

Here I am flanked by Lucien Rolland and Wilf Carter at Runnymede.

At the end of one of my trips to Wyoming.

Lee Wulff and I head outdoors again.

Two Brook Lodge on the Upsalquitch, New Brunswick, Canada, in midsummer.

Atlantic salmon in midair on my line.

With Basil Cheney and our
catch in the Adirondacks.

Runnymede camp, Restigouche River, New Brunswick, Canada.

Evening on the Restigouche, Deeside. I took this picture myself and like to have it around.

Wildlife Fund was organized in 1961 by some very far-sighted gentlemen, among them Luc Hoffman, the founder of Hoffman-LaRoche; David Ogilvy, one of the great pioneers in advertising; and Anton Rupert, a prominent South African whom I have known as a very able competitor in tobacco and a very concerned conservationist. Those people, with the help of Prince Bernhard of the Netherlands, conceived the idea that there should be something done about what was happening to our planet. I happened to be one of the original members of the World Wildlife Fund. We came together in the "Thousand and One Club," so called because each of 1,001 members pledged $10,000 to get the fund rolling. This was the first organized attempt on the part of leading people in the business world to do something about conservation.

At the time I was just an upstart CEO at small but growing Philip Morris, and it was a marvelous experience for me to be associated with these very senior executives in such a worthwhile endeavor. Almost from its inception, the World Wildlife Fund has been the leading organization in its field. It still is today the largest conservation organization in the world with 1.2 million members, and has undertaken more than 2,000 projects in 116 countries.

These projects range from initiating and supporting research into what endangered species require in order to survive, to lobbying for restrictions on the sale of animal parts, such as rhino horns, which are used as traditional medicines in the Far East, and elephant tusks for ivory. A century ago there were some 100,000 tigers in Asia; today the tigers number between 4,000 and 6,000 because of indiscriminate killing and habitat loss. The WWF has been involved in the preservation of the remaining tigers and the protection of the species for a quarter of a century, with good results. A few years ago it might have been necessary for me to explain just what the World Wildlife Funds does, but today it is a far more visible organization. If you have ever come across someone wearing a panda pin, that person is a member of the WWF. The endangered panda is our symbol.

The Fund's first president was Francis Kellogg. Then Dillon Ripley, the secretary of the Smithsonian, a great ornithologist, and important person in the WWF's early days, became the first U.S. WWF chairman. Russell Train, an early board member, wound up succeeding Ripley as chairman and became one of the Fund's most visible figures. He was director of the Environmental Protection Agency under Reagan and Bush and now is back at WWF as a most useful chairman emeritus. In the early days we supported the U.S. WWF out of my office in New York. My principal contribution has been getting people involved and getting whatever support I could for WWF, and I serve on the board to this day as its first honorary director.

I have also been involved in other conservation organizations, including the American Museum of Natural History, on whose board I've served for a quarter-century. In the post–World War II years it was a quiet, stuffy, unimaginative organization. Today, under the inspiring leadership of Ellen Futter it is dynamic, as exemplified by the new Roosevelt Rotunda restoration, the totally new Hayden Planetarium building (the Frederick and Sandra Rose Center for Earth and Space), and the complete rebuilding of the dinosaur exhibits. I also love the Bronx Zoo and under one of the great world conservationists, Bill Conway, it has become a leader in conservation and protection of endangered species worldwide and is now called the Wildlife Conservation Society.

I was introduced to East Africa in 1963 by Edward Lasker, a dear friend from Yale who later became a member of the PM board. One day he told me, "Joe, I know you love the outdoors. You should take a safari to East Africa with me." Lasker had been to Kenya in 1962 to watch the shooting of a Howard Hawks film, *Hatari!*, with John Wayne. Edward's experience led us to take the trip the following year to Nairobi and into the bush.

It was a marvelous experience, really an eye-opener. I had been exposed to the outdoors by my father, but that was mostly fishing. I had never before been to East Africa, or thought much about it, although I was raised within walking distance of the American Museum of Natural History, which has great African dioramas in Akeley Hall. In my youth I preferred playing in the streets or in Central Park to attending museums.

On my safaris—fourteen of them in all, almost every other year since 1963—I visited Kenya, Uganda, and Tanzania in East Africa. My professional hunter on my first hunting trip, and on most others I took, was Terry Mathews. Over the years he has become a dear friend. Once Terry took me out in early morning to shoot sand grouse in Kenya. He told me it was important to be at this water hole at eight A.M., and to keep very still. The sand grouse did come in at precisely eight—thousands of them. They circled the water hole, swooped down and scooped up a bit of water, and then flew away. I shot a dozen or so of them. We had delicious grouse for dinner that evening. Earlier that day while we were shooting birds, I heard a noise to one side, and there was a lion, feeding on a zebra, maybe a hundred yards away. Mathews told me not to worry; the lion was too occupied to bother with us.

East Africa is a unique part of the world. It has plains, deserts, beautiful swamps, waterfalls, mountains like Kilimanjaro, and extraordinary wildlife. It is positively mind-boggling. The Samburu and Turkana tribespeople are quite friendly, because they have become accustomed to people coming to see their country. The adults are about seven feet tall and very imposing. The many Masai warriors are impressive, too. In order to be accepted as a warrior, a Masai man has to kill a lion with a spear. I never saw one kill a lion, but I did manage to obtain a Masai spear to bring home as a memento.

My travel to East Africa troubled some members of the Philip Morris board in the 1960s. Often, I was in remote areas, out of touch with the rest of the world. What if some crisis developed and I couldn't be reached? Wasn't this East Africa business somewhat dangerous? So they placed some constraints on me. I was allowed to fly only on twin-engine planes, not single-engine planes, and the board required that there always be a co-pilot.

Once at Entebbe Airport I boarded a small chartered plane, but there was no co-pilot. I told the pilot we had ordered one, and he cheerily replied, "Mr. Cullman, *you* are the copilot." I had no choice but to get into the seat next to him, and off we went.

At 6,000 or 7,000 feet the pilot put the plane on automatic pilot, took out a copy of *Playboy*, and started to read. It was rather unnerving, especially since we were going over some wild territory. I glanced at the gas gauges and saw that one wing tank was empty and the other was close to it. I called this to the pilot's attention and he perked up. "Oh, thanks!" he shouted, and we landed immediately. Almost everything on these trips was interesting; there was always something new.

My very first trip to Africa was a photographic safari, but after that until the last few I mostly went hunting. On my first big-game-hunting trip my first shot was a Grant's gazelle, because Terry Mathews, my professional hunter, wanted to see how well I shot before we went after larger and more dangerous game. I must have passed the test, because then we went after cape buffalo. These are fast, dangerous, and tricky animals. Terry spotted one in the bush. How he did so was amazing, because when he pointed it out to me, all I could see was the glistening black nose about fifty yards away. I crawled forward, followed by the gun bearer, with Terry close behind.

The buffalo was in the bush, about thirty-five yards away. Terry whispered, "Take your time, but try to hit him in that glistening nose with the first shot." Otherwise the animal would charge, and then we would be in trouble. This one turned out all right.

In 1967 I shot an elephant near the Tana River, off the Indian Ocean in eastern Kenya. In those days the elephant population was being culled, because there were too many of them and they were destroying crops and other vegetation that meant life or death to human inhabitants. An elephant eats and eliminates 500 pounds of herbivorous material per day, so the impact of an elephant herd on the environment is major.

Elephants in those days were so plentiful that such culling had the support of environmental groups who understood the situation. Also, to shoot an elephant you had to obtain a license, the fee for which provided the government important revenues. The real threat to African wildlife was not and is not hunting, but rather is the growth of the human population competing for space with wildlife. This may sound strange to those who consider hunting unacceptable, but most people today know that hunters are conservationists and are largely responsible for the great resurgence of wildlife in North America where the whitetailed deer, an endangered species in Theodore Roosevelt's day has risen from 2,500 at the start of the century to more than 10 million today. I am very aware of the endangered status of African elephants today. The situation was quite different in 1967. I wouldn't consider shooting an elephant today.

Back then, more than thirty years ago, we were camped next to the Tana River, and every morning at daybreak we would get up and go to the river's edge and look for elephant tracks. An experienced tracker will have no trouble locating them, though some escaped me. When we started tracking the elephants we walked about twenty or twenty-five miles a day for three days in extreme heat. We finally came up to a bull elephant, but my hunter told me it was too small. Fifty-pound ivory tusks were good; seventy-five pounds was excellent. We finally came across three bulls, one of which turned out to have eighty-five-pound tusks.

The elephant was about fifty yards away. Terry Mathews had told me the best shot was the "brain shot" in the earhole, the elephant's most vulnerable point, but I couldn't get a shot off because the elephant turned and faced me directly. Terry whispered, "Is that big enough for you?" and I nodded. "You have to move to one side for the shot," he said, still whispering. But as we moved, the elephant turned, still looking straight at us. And then he charged, trumpeting loudly, ears out. His trunk was high in the air, and Terry said, "The chest shot." I'd never seen an elephant's chest before.

I had a Wetherby 470, which is a big, powerful rifle. I'm not a great shot, but I knew that if I didn't get the elephant with the first bullet things would become too interesting. I shot at twenty-five yards, and he fell at fifteen yards. Terry said, "Great shot," but then the elephant rose and started running away. Terry shouted, "Try the spine shot!" I aimed at the retreating elephant's rear and let go. My shot hit the mark, the elephant's rear. Terry said, "Great. We call that the exhaust shot." The elephant went down for good about 500 yards away. I ran up to the fallen elephant and dispatched him with one final bullet. I looked down. All I had on were my sneakers and jockey shorts. The "wait a bit" thorn trees had torn away my khaki shirt and shorts.

With this our bearers and others in the area went up to the elephant and started carving him up. We took the ivory; then they skinned the elephant to make bags and other equipment from the skins. The meat was eaten. Nothing was wasted.

East Africa has changed very much since I first went there in 1963. At that time there were 30,000 Europeans and 4.5 million Kenyans. The European population is the same today, but now there are around 28 million Kenyans. It is a primitive life once you get away from the big cities like Nairobi. In the countryside the Kenyans farm and hunt, and while the men look after their herds, the women do all the other work. Clitorectomies are still quite common, despite efforts to end this barbaric practice. Civilization as we know it has not helped very much. Young people are moving to the cities.

To address the wildlife problems in Tanzania, in 1990 I joined forces with the renowned professional hunter Robin Hurt, who runs Robin Hurt Safaris, to form the Cullman Wildlife Project (CWP). Some of the funding comes from a 20 percent surcharge Hurt imposes on those who use his hunting services in his government-designated areas or blocks in Tanzania, and I have helped raise money in the United States for its support.

The Cullman Wildlife Project employs local Tanzanians, mostly former poachers, who are organized into teams that search out and arrest poachers, confiscate their snares and poisoned arrows, and turn them in to the proper authorities. Since 1990 more than 20,000 snares have been recovered, saving the lives of an estimated 100,000 animals. Those local people are paid for their work—from $2.50 for small steel snares recovered and destroyed to $500 for an elephant or rhino poacher, armed with a rifle, who is arrested and prosecuted.

In general, licensed hunters kill only animals that are

abundant and that, if their numbers grow too large, may actually overgraze the area and threaten the existing wildlife. Poachers, on the other hand, kill indiscriminately and can decimate species. If you had gone to East Africa years ago, you would soon have learned just how many species were endangered. Some of these are thriving today, largely because of the reduction in snaring, illegal shooting, and other forms of poaching.

Tanzania is twice as large as California, with a population of only 28 million, almost all of whom are native East Africans representing more than a hundred different cultural groups. Tanzania has an average annual per capita income of approximately $260. This is a very poor country by any measure. There are some cash crops, such as coffee, cotton, and nuts, but the manufacturing sector is quite small.

Were it not for tourism and hunting, Tanzania would not have the funds to import machinery and transportation equipment so badly needed for development. Robin Hurt takes tourists and hunters on safaris, and uses part of the money they bring to Tanzania to help preserve the wildlife and the habitat so future tourists will want to go there.

The difference between a country like Tanzania and places like Singapore and Hong Kong is that Tanzania has natural riches but lacks an educated workforce and a relatively efficient government. The economy, too, is inefficient. There are waves of violence in East Africa that scare away tourists. The Cullman Wildlife Project is making a small contribution toward alleviating the problems and attracting more tourists.

The CWP makes life better for the Tanzanians and the people of other parts of East Africa. Under the CWP leadership of people like Michelle and Brian Connors and David Wallas, who have Peace Corps experience in the region, the CWP identifies and then funds worthwhile social projects in the Robin Hurt hunting blocks. These projects include digging wells and constructing water pipelines from sources into the villages, so that women will not have to walk ten or fifteen miles with full five-gallon cans on their heads to provide water for their families. There are health projects, aid to schools, and a maize mill.

This is a small operation, with an annual budget of around $250,000. I know that kind of money can't make a very large imprint on a large country, but it can point the way for others. Some government officials appreciate what we are doing, and that we are using CWP as a pilot program, hoping other conservation organizations active in Tanzania will expand the CWP idea to other parts of the country.

I have always hunted in the United States. For almost twenty-five years one of the highlights of my year has been a trip to the magnificent Bighorn Mountains on the Wyoming-Montana border just north of Sheridan, Wyoming. Sheridan still has many of the qualities of a frontier community; it's simple but grand, with a breathtaking view to the north and west of the snow-covered Bighorns. Visiting Sheridan has a way of turning the clock back to the days of Custer's Last Stand, which took place nearby, at the Little Bighorn River.

Overnight for a room and bath in a good hotel-motel in Sheridan still costs $36, and I recently hosted a fine dinner for ten there for $80. The men still wear their ten-gallon cowboy hats at dinner; western clothing predominates. It is rolling cattle country, but as the land slopes upward toward the foothills of the Bighorns game is plentiful. Pheasant, wild turkey, elk, mule or Western deer, white-tailed deer, coyote, and grouse are there to see and enjoy. The odd moose is seen, and the mountain lion is coming back.

I usually arrive in mid-October, in time for the opening day of elk and deer hunting season. I always have the appropriate nonresident license, which takes several months to obtain. These licenses are issued on a limited basis in the interests of conservation. To assure accuracy, we bore-sight our rifles the afternoon of arrival. I'm still using my fifty-year-old Winchester model 70-270, which has never back-fired in the United States or East Africa.

We have breakfast before dawn at Perkins Restaurant, then around 4:30 A.M. we drive slowly up the slope. We leave our vehicle below the coniferous forest line and trudge the rest of the way until we can hide behind a pine tree and search below us for elk or deer. We see the sun rise. It is a splendid, memorable experience. After the hunt on Lambert Niederinghaus' T Bar T ranch, we have a great lunch at his comfortable cabin on the slope around noon and plan for the next hunt for those who are not successful.

It's a truly unforgettable experience, especially for those of us who spend so much time dodging taxis, roller bladers, bicyclists, buses, and trucks in New York City. I've made some great friends in Sheridan including our hunting friends Bud Campbell and C.B. Elmgren; Val Shallcross, widow of my 1935 Yale classmate, John Shallcross; and Mercedes Kibbee, widow of the former CFO of Philip Morris who lives in Sheridan.

Conservation takes many forms. For some it is the preservation of endangered species; for others it may be the restoration of once-great architectural gems that become shabby and sad. Several years ago I had the opportunity to combine my lifelong enjoyment of tennis and the tennis world by helping in the restoration of one of these landmarks, the International Tennis Hall of Fame in Newport, Rhode Island.

Tennis is not quite as major a sport as baseball, basketball, football, and hockey, which draw huge crowds and often dominate the sports pages and TV limelight in their seasons. But tennis is big and deserves to be in the same league as golf. Both are participant sports people enjoy watching in person and on TV. I love to watch tennis and golf and I have played both for as long as I can remember. I have also developed a keen interest in the future of both sports.

I played my first golf at the Ruissemont Golf Club near Lake Placid in the Adirondacks. I was twelve years old. This was 1924. In 1929 I remember watching Bobby Jones sink a curving downhill putt to tie Al Espinosa at Winged Foot in the U.S. Open. Jones won the playoff easily the next day.

In the late 1930s, Ben Hogan was the assistant pro to Dan Mackie at the Century Country Club in Purchase, New York. I played in many pro-ams with Hogan. In those days he hit a low draw shot. He was quiet and determined and practiced endlessly. His hands were gnarled with calluses. He spoke little, but you felt his great character. Nelson Long, our present pro at Century, attributes whatever talent I have to watching and playing with Ben Hogan. It was a privilege.

In 1939, with a 12 handicap, I won the Lake Placid Amateur Championship at the Craig Wood course there. Match play. Then in early September the German march into Poland started World War II, and golf had to be put on hold for the duration, but I was the only officer on the cruiser *Montpelier* to bring his clubs to Australia. After World War II I got my handicap down to 4 and was twice a finalist (and lost) in the Century Club championship.

Golf is a great challenge—the toughest sport I played, both mentally and physically. I think my greatest round was in the Anderson Memorial at Winged Foot's west course. I played with Julian Frankel, a good friend from Ethical Culture days and the Century Club. I shot five natural birdies that day.

I've also played tennis my whole life. I became interested in tennis as a "project" in the 1960s, when the sport was dominated mostly by club types who played at restricted clubs. There were some public facilities, to be sure, but these were few and far between, and certainly didn't attract widespread lower- and middle-class participation. The country club perception of tennis dated from a time when male players wore flannel trousers and long-sleeved shirts and the women wore long dresses, and would flit from cocktails at umbrella-shaded tables to the courts. Had you talked to any of these people about popularizing tennis they would have thought you bizarre. Why bother? Everything was fine the way it was.

This was not an unusual attitude, nor was it confined to tennis. The players of my youth had been born into a world in which social class was a paramount consideration. There were proletarian sports such as baseball, basketball, and football, which could be played in the streets or on vacant lots with a minimum of equipment; and then there were upper-class sports, such as horse racing, golf, and tennis, which were for the well-to-do and those who aspired to such status.

As the nation democratized, especially after the Great Depression and World War II, the proletarian sports became more popular than the upper-class sports. The golfing people eventually began to wake up, and that sport is now so popular that the demand for golf courses exceeds the supply. Golf was slower than most to lower the color barriers, but I believe the advent of Tiger Woods will do for golf what my friend Arthur Ashe accomplished for tennis.

Now for my role in tennis, and my attempts to address some of the sport's problems. In 1968, I had become part of the tennis "establishment." I was active in helping get the U.S. Championship held at Forest Hills nationally televised for the first time on CBS and sponsored by Marlboro. This national TV broadcast of the U.S. championships changed tennis from a white shoe club sport to a sport for all Americans. In 1969 and again in 1970 I served as chairman of the U.S. Open with Owen Williams, a noted South African Davis Cup player, as director. In 1972 I would serve as co-chairman for the first Robert F. Kennedy Pro-Celebrity Tournament to support the activities of the Kennedy Memorial, which worked with underprivileged young people.

I was not happy with the lack of diversity—racial, religious, gender, and economic—of the players and those in the stands. There were a few outside the mold earlier—very few. One was Pancho Segura, who arrived in America from Ecuador in 1940 and was a strong competitor during that decade.

More change was on the way, in the form of Pancho Gonzales, Althea Gibson, Arthur Ashe, Manuel Santana, Billie Jean King, and a host of other minority and women players. It was something like the situation Jackie Robinson faced in baseball after the war. I appreciated that it takes time for people to change attitudes, but tennis wasn't moving fast enough until the Marlboro CBS-TV national sponsorship changed things.

Philip Morris had been a major advertiser and supporter of many sporting events, and this sponsorship helped our image. As I said we were the first TV sponsor of the U.S. tennis championships in 1968, 1969, and 1970, and achieved good ratings on CBS. All this might be amazing to latecomers to the sport. Tennis is so popular today, not only among players, but with viewers as well, but that wasn't the case back then.

The birth of the Virginia Slims Tour was instrumental in popularizing the sport. When Virginia Slims began sponsoring women's tennis in 1970 a women's professional tour was nonexistent. The women players played either for expenses only or for nothing at all. Tennis was a male-dominated sport, and the men playing in the major tour sanctioned by the United States Lawn Tennis Association (USLTA, later the USTA) were the only players earning top prize money.

The women players called for recognition in the form of prize money. The issue boiled up in the fall of 1970, just before the USLTA–sanctioned Pacific Southwest tournament in Los Angeles. The tournament was run by former tennis great Jack Kramer, who had been U.S. singles champion in 1946 and 1947.

Inspired by Gladys Heldman, the founder, editor, and publisher of *World Tennis* magazine, and led by Billie Jean King, the number one woman player in the world at the time, nine women players demanded that the discrepancy between men's and women's prize money be addressed. Kramer refused to consider their demand and told them that they would be subject to suspension by the USLTA and to the loss of their eligibility cards if they did not play in the Pacific Southwest tournament.

The women held their ground and Gladys Heldman offered to run a women's event in Houston, Texas, opposite Kramer's Los Angeles tournament. The women's tournament, to be held at the Houston Racquet Club, was originally to be called the Houston Invitational, but when Gladys—who was a good friend of mine—told me what was going on and that she was looking for corporate support, I saw a unique opportunity to support women's tennis.

As I've mentioned, Philip Morris had just been the first national sponsor on CBS-TV of the U.S. Championship at Forest Hills. I saw the Houston tournament as a chance to support the women's game and as a unique sponsorship opportunity for Philip Morris. So we put up $2,500 and had the name of the event changed to the Virginia Slims Invitational. The tournament, which had total prize money of $7,500, was won by Rosie Casals and marked the birth of the women's professional tennis tour.

The USLTA responded by taking away the eligibility cards of those players who competed in Houston, which meant they could no longer play in USLTA sanctioned events. Billie Jean King, Rosie Casals, and the other players countered by signing contracts with Gladys Heldman—for one dollar. Within a week after the first Virginia Slims Invitational in November 1970, we were able to announce that Virginia Slims would sponsor eight women's tournaments, each in a sixteen-draw format beginning in January 1971. And the rest is tennis history.

By the end of 1971 there were sixty-four women competing in tournaments for about $225,000. In 1972, with Virginia Slims' continued support, two $100,000 events took place, one in Boca Raton, Florida, and the other in Hilton Head, South Carolina. That same year Billie Jean King became the first female athlete in history to win $100,000 in prize money—a lot of money at that time—in a single year.

A year later, in 1973, King became a household name when she defeated Bobby Riggs in "The Battle of the Sexes," the most watched tennis match of all time and an event that brought women into the forefront of athletics. I attended that match in Houston, Texas. As Ted Tinling, the noted tennis fashion designer and tennis historian said of the match in his book *Sixty Years in Tennis*, "Previously Joe had been a lone prophet of marrying big business with women's tennis. Now big business was dotted all the way around the arena, sharing in a media happening of gargantuan proportions."

King was a leader in getting the women's tour under way, and she fought for equality in women's tennis. Then players like Chris Evert and Evonne Goolagong heightened the awareness and interest in the sport, and Chris's legendary rivalry with Martina Navratilova provided an exciting story line for women's tennis for many years. The Virginia Slims Tour, which culminated annually with the women's championship at Madison Square Garden, became one of the most successful promotions in women's sports history and lasted for more than twenty years.

Because of my involvement in the Virginia Slims Tour and

my overall love of the sport, it was only natural that I would become connected with the International Tennis Hall of Fame. Anyone with an interest in tennis and a knowledge of architecture knows about the International Tennis Hall of Fame in Newport, Rhode Island. In the late 1970s the facility, which was then nearly a century old, was falling down, literally. Had this situation been allowed to continue, there would be no beautiful International Tennis Hall of Fame today.

Visitors to the facility today will see a fine structure designed by Stanford White across the street from a large shopping center. The structure was built over a century ago, in 1881, as "the Newport Casino." The Newport Casino had been established by *New York Herald* publisher James Gordon Bennett, Jr., when he was denied membership in another exclusive club there, the Reading Room. Irate at this treatment, Bennett commissioned McKim, Mead & White, the most renowned architectural firm of the day, to design what was to be the Casino.

Stanford White himself, a world celebrity architect, was the lead person on this project. The club quickly became the social center for American aristocrats when they summered at their Newport "cottages." From its opening in 1881 through 1914, it was the site of the men's U.S. National Championship, played on grass. The younger people played tennis there as well, but mostly this was a sport for wealthy amateurs.

This was still the case with tennis in 1954, when James Van Allen founded the Tennis Hall of Fame at the by then dilapidated Casino. But things were changing, especially after 1970 when tennis grew in popularity. The wealthy amateurs were still on the scene, but were joined by professionals with names like Bobby Riggs, Roy Emerson, Billie Jean King, and Chris Evert. Which was where I came in.

I knew many of the big names in the sport, and so was approached for assistance in helping to rebuild and restore the Tennis Hall of Fame. I wanted to help out a worthy artistic and cultural force in the community. I hoped visits there would inspire young people to play tennis, learn its history, and glorify the great players of the past.

The thought of restoring Bennett's building in Newport was very appealing. So together with friends, associates, and those who felt as I did about tennis, I assisted the Hall of Fame in meeting its $7.5 million capital goal. William Mc-Chesney Martin, one of the great names in American finance and public service, who is best known for his long tenure as chairman of the Federal Reserve Board, was particularly helpful in the early years. His wife is Cynthia Davis, whose family gave the Davis Cup, one of the premier trophies in tennis.

One of the architectural features of the building is its clock tower, which I'm proud to say has been named the Cullman Clock Tower. Seeing it provides me with great pleasure whenever I go to Newport events, and the restored Hall of Fame is a much sought-after site for a wide variety of social events, including one of my 1935 Yale mini-reunions. I always say to Jane Brown, our marvelous ITHF president, "The casino looks better today than it did over one hundred years ago."

WHILE IT MIGHT APPEAR from all I've said here that I was leading an ideal life—successful in business, active in sports, and contributing to international wildlife conservation, my life in the early 1970s had become somewhat emotionally confused and difficult.

During the fall of 1973 I began to see a good deal of Joan Paley Straus, a very attractive woman almost twenty years my junior. I had known Joan socially for many years when we were both members of the Century Club. We'd see each other at parties when she was married to Barney Straus. She was much younger, very pretty, and a good athlete.

This relationship led to a very difficult emotional problem for me and for her. I had strong bonds to my first wife but I found Joan dazzling. Later I moved to the Carlyle Hotel in New York and started the very difficult process of becoming separated from Sue. At this time I did not realize what a difficult move this would prove to be. My connections to my first family and friends were deep and of long standing. Sue and I had been married in 1935.

In February 1974, after becoming engaged, Joan and I visited East Hampton and decided to buy a Charles Gwathmey–built beach house there overlooking Hook Pond. We planned to get married after we were both divorced. We were married at our new house on Terbell Lane on September 22, 1974, a lovely day with swans flying overhead. Lots of family from both sides, including Joan's two children, Barney Junior and Tracy, were in attendance. But later that fall I was back at the Carlyle, unable to adjust to my new life and to living at Joan's apartment on East Sixty-sixth Street.

It was not a good time for me, and this vacillation lasted for many years during which we kept seeing each other a great deal but remained in an uncertain marital status. We were happily remarried on January 23, 1988, ten years ago. It was a most difficult period for both of us, but we now have a lovely penthouse apartment in the East Seventies in Manhattan and a house near Montego Bay, Jamaica, as well as the East Hampton house. And love prevailed. Joan and I are very happy. One of her passions is the theater, and I learned to love it. She now loves the outdoors—in small doses and when the right people are with her.

I'm a lucky guy in so many ways—family, friends, health, career—but more extraordinary than any of these is my good luck in being around at eighty-five and being able to give back to society and nature so much of the monetary good fortune that has come my way. It seems to me that the success of a capitalistic, democratic society depends so much on its citizens' dedication to philanthropy. It's a responsibility that successful American businessmen must fulfill with generosity.

I suppose that when my obituaries are written they will stress my work at Philip Morris, and I have no quarrel with that. But a person is more than his work. I consider my efforts at conservation through the World Wildlife Fund, the Atlantic Salmon Federation, and the International Tennis Hall of Fame to have been a most important part of my life. My involvement and support of activities at Hotchkiss and Yale were another important part of my life. Also my family and friends have been a source of great happiness. Without all these I would have been much less fulfilled and would have accomplished less.

Thinking back about my life and looking back on the pages and pictures in this book, I realize what a lucky guy I have been.

# Index